LONGMAN

SOCIAL STUDIES

WORKBOOK

Longman

Longman Social Studies
Workbook

Thanks to Roberto E. Yarzagaray for his contribution.

Pearson Education, 10 Bank Street, White Plains, NY 10606

Vice president, primary and secondary editorial: Ed Lamprich
Senior development editor: Virginia Bernard
Development editor: Deborah Maya Lazarus
Editorial coordinator: Johnnie Farmer
Editorial assistant: Emily Lippincott
Vice president, director of production and design: Rhea Banker
Production supervisor: Christine Edmonds
Associate managing editor: Jane Townsend
Vice president, marketing: Kate McLoughlin
Senior marketing manager: Don Wulbrecht
Senior manufacturing buyer: Nancy Flaggman

Cover design: Rhea Banker
Cover Photo Credits: (background) Art Resource, N.Y.; (top row left to right) Royalty-Free/Corbis,
Jonathan Blair/Corbis, Francisco Cruz/SuperStock, Prentice Hall School Division; (top left)
Hisham F. Ibrahim/Getty Images, (top right) Fine Art Photographic Library/Corbis,
(bottom left) Tom Stack & Associates, Inc., (bottom right) Dorling Kindersley Media
Library; (back cover) Garry Gay/Getty Images.

Text design and composition: Quarasan
Text font: 11/14 ITC Franklin Gothic Book
Credits: See page 135.

LONGMAN ON THE **WEB**

Longman.com offers online resources for
teachers and students. Access our Companion
Websites, our online catalog, and our local
offices around the world.

Visit us at **longman.com**.

ISBN: 0-13-193027-3

Printed in the United States of America
2 3 4 5 6 7 8 9 10–BAH–09 08 07 06

Contents

Getting Started: Introduction

Unit 1: Early Civilizations

Lesson ❶

Before You Read 17

More Review and Practice 21

Lesson ❷

Before You Read 23

More Review and Practice 27

Unit Review 29

Unit 2: The Classical World

Lesson 1

Lesson 2

Unit 3: The Middle Ages

Lesson 1

Contents

Contents

Unit 5: Early United States

Lesson ❶

Lesson ❷

Unit 6: A New Nation

Lesson ❶

Lesson ❷

Unit 7: The Modern World

Lesson ❶

Lesson ②

Getting Started: Introduction

What Is Social Studies?

VOCABULARY

A. Match the parts of the sentence. Write the letter.

_____f_____ **1.** Social studies   **a.** is the study of the past.

_____ **2.** Society   **b.** is the way money, goods, and services are made and used.

_____ **3.** Geography   **c.** is the people who control what happens in a country.

_____ **4.** Economics   **d.** is the study of oceans, mountains, countries, and weather.

_____ **5.** History   **e.** is a group of people in the same country with the same customs.

_____ **6.** Government   **f.** is history, geography, economics, and government.

B. Complete each sentence. Use words from the box.

economics	geography	history	social studies	government

1. _____ helps us learn about other countries and the weather.

2. The United States _____ is a democracy.

3. _____ helps us learn about goods and services.

4. _____ helps us learn facts about people and places in the past.

5. In _____ we learn many things about a society.

C. Circle the word or phrase that doesn't belong.

1. money   economics   (voters)   services

2. history   weather   past   study

3. democracy   voters   government   oceans

4. buy   countries   geography   mountains

5. society   people   customs   weather

6. social studies   science   history   geography

D. Circle the best word to complete each sentence.

1. Clothes and food are examples of (services / goods).

2. Schools and hospitals are examples of (services / trade).

3. In the study of history, we learn about the (past / future).

4. (Government / Trade) is when people buy or sell goods or services.

5. In the study of geography, we learn about (weather / money).

E. Write T for *true* or F for *false*.

_____ 1. *Democratic* means that people cannot choose their leaders.

_____ 2. Economics is the study of the ways that money, goods, and services are made and used.

_____ 3. When we study social studies, we learn about plants and animals.

_____ 4. A society is a group of governments.

_____ 5. A country's geography can influence its history.

F. Write words from the box under the correct category.

past	money	vote	democracy
leaders	weather	mountains	goods

Economics	Geography	History	Government
1. _____	1. _____	1. _____	1. _____
2. _____	2. _____		2. _____
			3._____

Getting Started: Introduction

What Is Social Studies?

VOCABULARY

Complete the chart below. Write three more parts of social studies.

Social Studies

History

The Five Themes of Geography

A. Complete the puzzle. Write the secret word.

1. It tells you where a place is.

   __ Ⓞ __ __ __ __ __ __

2. It is a description of the physical and human characteristics of the area.

   __ __ __ Ⓞ __

3. It is how people, things, and ideas move from one place to another.

   __ __ __ Ⓞ __ __ __ __

4. It is how people affect the world around them.

   __ __ __ __ __ Ⓞ __ __ __ __ __

5. It is an area that shares at least one feature with another area.

   __ __ __ __ __ Ⓞ

   Secret word: __ __ __ __ __

B. Draw an arrow between words that are related. Then write five sentences with those words.

Location	common features
Region	a place
Geography	affects the world
Place	five themes
Movement	different climate, landforms, or plants
Interaction	from one place to another

Example: _Location tells you where a place is._

1. _____

2. _____

3. _____

4. _____

5. _____

Name _____ Date _____

Getting Started: Introduction

Geographic Terms

A. Match the words in Column A with the definitions in Column B. Write the letter.

Column A	Column B
_____ **1.** mountain	**a.** one of the large areas of land on the earth
_____ **2.** hemisphere	**b.** a low area of land where a river divides
_____ **3.** climate	**c.** an area of very high land, a high hill
_____ **4.** continent	**d.** an area of low land between hills or mountains
_____ **5.** ocean	**e.** a part of the ocean with land on three sides of it
_____ **6.** valley	**f.** a large area of water with land all around it
_____ **7.** plain	**g.** a pattern of weather in a place over a long time
_____ **8.** lake	**h.** a very large area of salt water
_____ **9.** delta	**i.** flat land
_____ **10.** gulf	**j.** half of the earth

B. Match the words in Column A with the definitions in Column B. Write the letter.

Column A	Column B
_____ **1.** coast	**a.** a hot and dry large area of land
_____ **2.** peninsula	**b.** a part of an ocean enclosed by a curve in the land
_____ **3.** canyon	**c.** a mountain with a hole at the top
_____ **4.** bay	**d.** a deep valley with steep sides
_____ **5.** hill	**e.** a piece of land surrounded by water
_____ **6.** river	**f.** an area of salt water, smaller than an ocean
_____ **7.** desert	**g.** a small mountain
_____ **8.** island	**h.** a continuous flow of fresh water
_____ **9.** sea	**i.** the land next to a sea or ocean
_____ **10.** volcano	**j.** a piece of land with water on three sides

C. Look at the map. Write the geographic terms next to the numbers on the map.

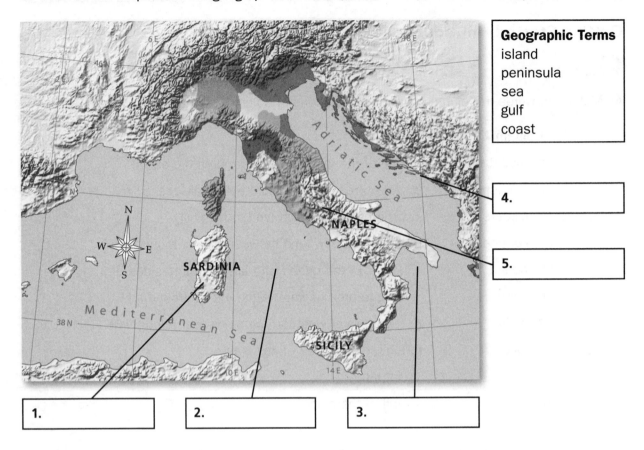

Geographic Terms
island
peninsula
sea
gulf
coast

4. _____

5. _____

1. _____

2. _____

3. _____

Getting Started: Introduction

Globes and Maps

MAPS

A. Look at the maps of Africa on pages 17 and 21 in your Student Book. Use those maps to choose the best answer to complete each sentence. Circle the letter.

1. The physical map of Africa shows _____.

   a. names of countries   **b.** elevation   **c.** cities

2. The physical map of Africa does not show _____.

   a. mountains   **b.** rivers   **c.** cities

3. The political map of Africa shows _____.

   a. names of mountains   **b.** national borders   **c.** elevation

4. The political map of Africa does not show _____.

   a. deserts   **b.** capitals   **c.** names of countries

5. Most countries in East Africa border the _____.

   a. Atlantic Ocean   **b.** Mediterranean Sea   **c.** Indian Ocean

6. The Cape of Good Hope is located in the _____.

   a. south   **b.** north   **c.** west

7. The Atlas Mountains are located in the _____.

   a. west   **b.** north   **c.** south

8. _____ Africa has many small countries.

   a. North   **b.** South   **c.** West

9. Mount Kilimanjaro is on the border of _____.

   a. Angola and Namibia   **b.** Tanzania and Kenya   **c.** Algeria and Libya

10. Madagascar is _____.

    a. a mountain   **b.** a river   **c.** an island

B. Look at the map of the world on pages 22–23 in your Student Book. Then answer the questions.

1. Name three countries in Asia.

_____

2. What is the capital of Canada?

_____

3. What countries border Peru?

_____

4. What country is south of Saudi Arabia?

_____

5. On what continent is Nigeria?

_____

C. Look at the map of the world. Write T for *true* or F for *false*.

_____ 1. China is in Asia.

_____ 2. Mexico is west of Central America.

_____ 3. Hawaii is in the Pacific Ocean.

_____ 4. Europe is west of Asia.

_____ 5. Greenland is near Antarctica.

_____ 6. Manila is the capital of Japan.

_____ 7. Alaska is part of the United States.

_____ 8. Paraguay is south of Argentina.

_____ 9. Nairobi is the capital of Kenya.

_____ 10. Brazil is a large country.

Getting Started: Introduction

Using Timelines, Charts, and Graphs

TIMELINES AND CHARTS

A. Look at the timeline about Mount Everest. Then answer the questions.

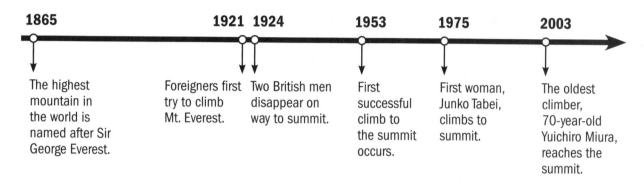

| 1865 | 1921 | 1924 | 1953 | 1975 | 2003 |

The highest mountain in the world is named after Sir George Everest.

Foreigners first try to climb Mt. Everest.

Two British men disappear on way to summit.

First successful climb to the summit occurs.

First woman, Junko Tabei, climbs to summit.

The oldest climber, 70-year-old Yuichiro Miura, reaches the summit.

1. When was the first successful climb to the summit of Mount Everest?

   _____

2. Who was the first woman to climb to the summit? When did she do that?

   _____

3. When did the oldest climber reach the summit?

   _____

4. When did two British men disappear on Mount Everest?

   _____

5. Who is Mount Everest named for? When did it receive that name?

   _____

B. Write T for *true* or F for *false*.

_____ **1.** Timelines show important events over a period of time.

_____ **2.** A chart is the same as a map.

_____ **3.** Two kinds of graphs are a line graph and a date graph.

_____ **4.** A flowchart is one kind of timeline.

_____ **5.** Charts can have rows and columns.

C. Read the chart of major battles and events in World War II. Then answer the questions.

Major Events in World War II		
Battle/Event	**Location**	**Date**
Battle of Britain	Great Britain	July–October, 1940
Japan bombs Pearl Harbor	Hawaii	December 7, 1941
Allies attack Germans in North Africa	North Africa	November, 1942
D-Day invasion	France	June 6, 1944
Battle of the Bulge	French-German-Belgian border	December 16, 1944
German government surrenders	Europe	May 7, 1945
Atomic bombing of Hiroshima and Nagasaki	Japan	August 6 and 9, 1945
Japan surrenders	Tokyo, Japan	September 2, 1945

1. What is the title of this chart?

_____

2. What years does the chart show?

_____

3. When did Japan bomb Pearl Harbor?

_____

4. When did the Germans surrender?

_____

5. When did the Japanese surrender?

_____

Getting Started: Introduction

Using Timelines, Charts, and Graphs

GRAPHS

This graph shows different groups of whites in the southern United States in 1860. Study the graph. Then answer the questions.

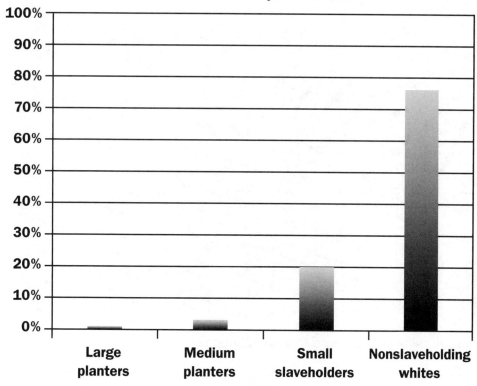

Southern White Population in 1860

1. Is this graph a bar graph or a line graph?

   _____

2. What year does this graph show?

   _____

3. Which groups were less than 10 percent of the white population?

   _____

4. Which group was 76 percent of the white population?

   _____

5. What percent were the small slaveholders?

   _____

Using Primary Sources

This is part of the original United States Constitution. It is a primary source. Look at the photo. Then answer the questions.

1. When do you think people wrote this Constitution?

   _____

2. What materials did they use to write it?

   _____

3. What words do you see on the Constitution?

   _____

4. Who are the people in "We the People"?

   _____

Unit 1: Lesson 1

Before You Read

VOCABULARY

A. Match the key words with a definition. Write the letter.

_____c_____ crops   **a.** large areas of ice

_____ **1.** hunter-gatherers   **b.** system of watering crops

_____ **2.** glaciers   **c.** plants that farmers grow

_____ **3.** archaeologist   **d.** raising animals and growing plants

_____ **4.** irrigation   **e.** early humans

_____ **5.** agriculture   **f.** scientist who looks for tools, pottery, and
                                          human bones

B. Write five sentences using a key word and its definition.

Example: _Crops are plants that farmers grow._ _____

1. _____
_____

2. _____

3. _____

4. _____

5. _____

C. Circle the best word to complete each sentence.

1. Early humans used rivers for (irrigation / glaciers).

2. (Hunter-gatherers / Archaeologists) look for places where people lived a long time ago.

3. Early humans grew (glaciers / crops) to eat.

4. (Agriculture / Irrigation) is growing crops and raising animals.

5. Early humans were (archaeologists / hunter-gatherers).

6. A long time ago (crops / glaciers) covered much of the earth.

Content Reading Strategy: Preview

A. Look at pages 38–39 in your Student Book and answer the questions.

1. What are the titles on these pages?

   _____

2. What are some important words on these pages? How do you know that they are important?

   _____

3. What do you see in the pictures?

   _____

   _____

4. The titles, pictures, captions, and vocabulary help you to know what this reading is about. What do you think you will learn about on these pages?

   _____

   _____

B. Preview the headings in Reading 1 in your Student Book. Write the headings below.

   1. _____

   2. _____

   3. _____

   4. _____

   5. _____

   6. _____

   7. _____

Unit 1: Lesson 1

Before You Read

SOCIAL STUDIES SKILLS

Using Visuals: Use a Timeline

Look at the timeline and pictures. Then answer the questions.

6600 B.C.E.   **5000** B.C.E.   **3500** B.C.E.   **2500** B.C.E.

People make
bronze   Rice grown in   Wheel invented   First libraries
                      southeast Asia   in Egypt

1. What event is first on the timeline?

   _____

2. What event is last on the timeline?

   _____

3. What event happened in 3500 B.C.E.?

   _____

4. How many years does this timeline cover?

   _____

5. When did they grow rice in southeast Asia?

   _____

Using Visuals: Use a Timeline

A. Make a timeline below. Write the following dates and events in the correct chronological order.

- 6000 B.C.E. Wheat farming spreads in the Nile Valley and Africa
- 8000 B.C.E. Towns develop in Middle East
- 4000 B.C.E. Farming begins in central Europe
- 7000 B.C.E. Farming begins in Mesopotamia
- 6600 B.C.E. People begin to make bronze tools

> Remember that in the B.C.E. time period, the years decrease (go from high to low).

8000 B.C.E.

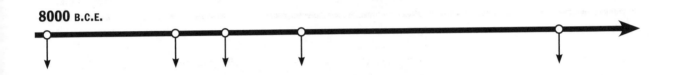

B. Answer the questions about the timeline.

1. What event is last on the timeline? What is the date?

   _____

2. How many years are there between the first event and the second event?

   _____

3. Which two events happened closely together?

   _____

4. Which two events happened 600 years apart?

   _____

5. What happened in 7000 B.C.E.?

   _____

Unit 1   Early Civilizations

Unit 1: Lesson 1

More Review and Practice

VOCABULARY

Complete the puzzle. Use key words. Write the secret word.

1. growing crops and raising animals   ___ ___ ___ ___ ___ ___ (O) ___ ___ ___

2. watering crops   ___ ___ ___ ___ ___ ___ ___ (O) ___

3. scientist who studies the past   ___ ___ ___ ___ ___ (O) ___ ___ ___ ___ ___

4. large areas of ice   ___ ___ (O) ___ ___ ___ ___ ___ ___

5. plants that a farmer grows   ___ ___ ___ ___ (O)

Secret word: ___ ___ ___ ___ ___

VOCABULARY IN CONTEXT

Complete each sentence. Use words from the box. There is one extra word.

hunter-gatherers	crops	glaciers
irrigation	agriculture	archaeologist

1. Farmers in dry areas use _____ to water their crops.

2. An _____ digs up ancient places to look for tools and pottery.

3. _____ are found in many cold places in the world.

4. Farmers in Mexico grow _____ such as corn, soybeans, rice, and beans.

5. _____ hunted animals and gathered plants.

TIMELINE CHECK

Use the timelines on pages 36–43 in your Student Book to answer the questions.

1. When did Hammurabi build a new empire?

   _____

2. What events happened in 1500 B.C.E.?

   _____

3. When was the first dictionary written in China?

   _____

Choose the best answer. Circle the letter.

1. Two important civilizations in Mesopotamia were _____.

   a. Sumer and Egypt   b. Phoenicia and Nineveh   c. Babylonia and Assyria

2. The Sumerians developed a system of writing called _____.

   a. Phoenician   b. cuneiform   c. battering rams

3. Early farmers lived near _____.

   a. rivers   b. glaciers   c. mountains

4. During the Stone Age, early humans made _____ from stone.

   a. clothes   b. tools   c. crops

5. People used metal to make tools during the _____.

   a. Ice Age   b. Stone Age   c. Bronze Age

APPLY SOCIAL STUDIES SKILLS

Content Reading Strategy: Preview

This is a map you will see in Lesson 2. Look at the map. Then answer the questions.

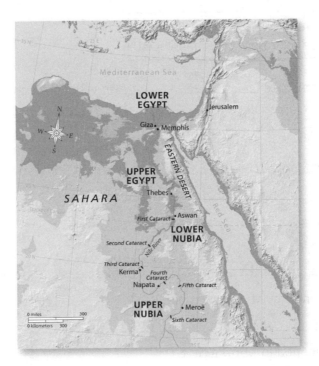

1. What seas do you see on the map? _____

2. What desert do you see? _____

3. What regions do you see? _____

4. Is this a map of Egypt today or a long time ago? _____

Unit 1: Lesson 2

Before You Read

VOCABULARY

A. Circle the best word to complete each sentence.

   1. (Invaders / Pyramids) were places to bury pharaohs.

   2. There were three (classes / rulers) of people in Egypt.

   3. Egyptian civilization is very (ancient / society).

   4. Some civilizations built walls to protect them from (classes / invaders).

   5. A (ruler / society) of a civilization is its leader.

   6. Egyptian (ruler / society) was divided into three classes of people.

B. Draw an arrow between words that are related. Write three sentences to tell how they are related.

ruler	pyramid	society	invaders
classes	pharaoh	slaves	walls

Example: _A pharaoh was a ruler._

   1. _____

   2. _____

   3. _____

C. Write T for *true* or F for *false*.

   _____ **1.** Classes are people who take over a country by force.

   _____ **2.** A society is a group of people living together.

   _____ **3.** Pyramids took twenty years to build.

   _____ **4.** A ruler is a slave.

   _____ **5.** Early civilizations are ancient.

   _____ **6.** Invaders built walls.

Content Reading Strategy: Predict

Look at the picture. Think about who these people are and what they are doing. Predict what will probably happen next. Write or draw three predictions.

Prediction 1

Prediction 2

Prediction 3

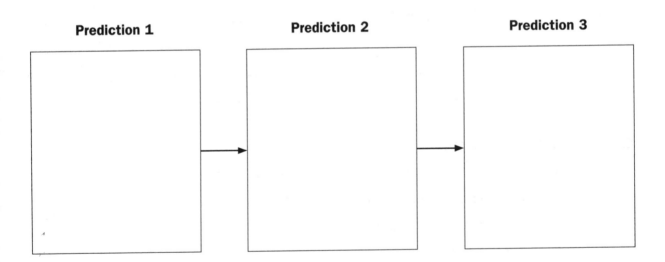

Unit 1: Lesson 2

Before You Read

Content Reading Strategy: Predict

Look at the picture. Then answer the questions.

1. Who is this person?

   _____

2. What is she looking for?

   _____

3. What will she find? Make three predictions.

   • _____

   • _____

   • _____

Using Visuals: Use a Timeline

A. Look at the important events in the history of writing. Write the dates and events in correct chronological order on the timeline. (c. = circa, or around that time)

- c. 550 B.C.E. Appearance of writing from left to right
- c. 3000 B.C.E. Sumerians create first writing system
- c. 750 B.C.E. Development of first Indian writing system
- c. 1000 B.C.E. Earliest samples of Phoenician writing
- c. 2500 B.C.E. Ink first used in Egypt and China
- c. 1300 B.C.E. Chinese make and use simple books

3000 B.C.E.

B. Answer the questions about the timeline.

1. What event is first on the timeline?

_____

2. How many years are there between the second event and the third event?

_____

3. In what year did people begin to write from left to right?

_____

4. What happened around 1300 B.C.E.?

_____

5. Where was ink first used?

_____

Name _____ Date _____

Unit 1: Lesson 2
More Review and Practice

VOCABULARY

Match the parts of the sentence. Write the letter.

_____ 1. A pyramid was built

_____ 2. Egyptian civilization

_____ 3. Assyrian invaders

_____ 4. The people in ancient China

_____ 5. An emperor

_____ 6. A group of people living together

a. is very ancient.

b. form a society.

c. divided their society into classes.

d. as a tomb for a pharaoh.

e. attacked the Nubians.

f. is a ruler.

VOCABULARY IN CONTEXT

Complete the paragraph. Use words from the box.

| ruler | class | society | ancient |

(1) _____ Chinese (2) _____ was based on farming. The Shang dynasty was the first dynasty in China to develop. This dynasty built the first cities and produced the first writing system. The (3) _____ of the Shang dynasty was the emperor. The emperor's family was part of the ruling (4) _____. There were other levels of society as well. The family was very important in early Chinese society. Many relatives lived together in extended families.

TIMELINE CHECK

Use the timelines on pages 50–57 in your Student Book to answer the questions.

1. When did the Middle Kingdom begin in Egypt?

_____

2. What happened in 700 B.C.E.?

_____

3. When was Confucius born?

_____

Unit 1 Early Civilizations

27

Read the sentences. Write T for *true* or F for *false*.

_____ **1.** The Egyptians developed picture symbols called hieroglyphics.

_____ **2.** In Nubia, people buried their kings in pyramids.

_____ **3.** Ancient Egypt was divided into three time periods called classes.

_____ **4.** The Egyptians were the first people to use a 365-day calendar.

_____ **5.** Confucius was a famous teacher from ancient Persia.

Content Reading Strategy: Predict

The ancient pyramids in Egypt are still standing today. Predict what will happen to the pyramids in the next 100 years. Write your prediction below.

_____

_____

_____

Using Visuals: Use a Timeline

Read the events on the following timeline. Then answer the questions.

Ancient Nubia

1600 B.C.E.	1500 B.C.E.	700 B.C.E.	600 B.C.E.	250 C.E.
Nubians push into Eygpt.	Nubia and Eygpt go to war; Eygpt wins.	Nubia gains independence from Egypt.	Nubians move capital to Meroë.	Meroë weakens and falls to Axum Kingdom.

1. Which event happened first?

_____

2. What happened after Nubia gained independence from Eygpt?

_____

3. In what year did Meroë fall?

_____

Unit 1:

Unit Review

VOCABULARY

Choose a word from the box to replace the words in *italics*. Write that word on the line.

irrigation	ancient	crops	ruler	archaeologists
invaders	glaciers	society	pyramids	

Example: Early farmers grew *plants* such as corn, rice, and wheat. _____crops_____

1. The Great Wall of China kept out *people who wanted to take over the country.* _____

2. Hatshepsut was the first woman *pharaoh* in Egypt. _____

3. We are learning about *very old* civilizations. _____

4. Emperors ruled the *group of people living together* in China. _____

5. *Scientists who look for ancient places* found tombs inside the pyramids.

   _____

6. *Ancient Egyptian tombs* are still standing today. _____

7. *Large pieces of ice* once covered a lot of the earth. _____

8. People used water from the rivers for *watering crops.* _____

VOCABULARY IN CONTEXT

Correct any false sentences on the lines below.

Example: Crops once covered much of the earth.
   Glaciers once covered much of the earth.

1. Hunter-gatherers grew crops and raised animals.

   _____

2. Glaciers were buried in pyramids.

   _____

3. Early societies had different classes: lower, middle, and upper.

   _____

4. In ancient China the family was very important to the invaders.

   _____

Put the events in the correct order. Number them from 1 to 6.

_____ Sumerians created cuneiform writing.

_____ Phoenician civilization developed.

_____ Nubians gained independence from Egypt.

_____ Persian king Cyrus united the Persians and Medes into one kingdom.

___/___ People learned to make bronze.

_____ Zhou dynasty began in China.

APPLY SOCIAL STUDIES SKILLS

Content Reading Strategies: Preview and Predict

Look at the picture and caption below. They are from the next unit (Unit 2). Make two predictions about what you will learn in Unit 2.

▲ Greek artists and builders made monuments such as temples to honor their gods. This monument is the Parthenon in Athens.

1. _____

   _____

2. _____

   _____

EXTENSION PROJECT

It is the year 2505, about 500 years into the future. An archaeologist finds a buried civilization. Draw a picture to show what kinds of things the archaeologist finds. Then tell about your picture.

Unit 1

Writing Skills

MAKE A PLAN

A. Look at the information about Hatshepsut on page 52 in your Student Book. Choose important details to add to the word web below. Add more boxes if needed.

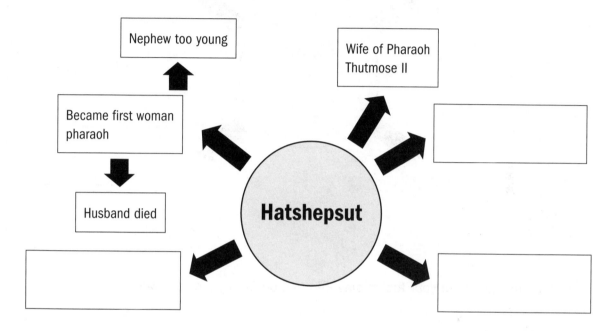

Nephew too young

Wife of Pharaoh Thutmose II

Became first woman pharaoh

Husband died

Hatshepsut

B. Write a paragraph below about Hatshepsut. Use your own words and details from the word web.

C. Now you are ready to plan a new topic. Choose a topic from the box, find information, and make a word web below. Add more boxes if needed.

Topics
Discovery of fire
Early tools
Ice Age homes
Cave paintings
The Great Wall of China

Topic:

D. Write a paragraph about your topic using information from your word web.

Unit 2: Lesson 1

Before You Read

VOCABULARY

A. Match the key words with a definition. Write the letter.

_____ **1.** drama   **a.** temples or other buildings to honor gods

_____ **2.** pottery   **b.** a play acted out for people

_____ **3.** festivals   **c.** figures made from marble

_____ **4.** sculptures   **d.** a large outdoor theater

_____ **5.** amphitheater   **e.** everyday items made from clay

_____ **6.** monuments   **f.** celebrations

B. Write four sentences using a key word and its definition.

1. _____

2. _____

3. _____

4. _____

C. Circle the best word to complete each sentence.

1. The ancient Greeks made (amphitheaters / monuments) to honor their gods.

2. (Pottery / Drama) was made from clay.

3. (Drama / Sculpture) was a part of many celebrations.

4. People watched plays in the (sculpture / amphitheater).

5. Greek artists made (sculptures / festivals) out of marble rock.

D. Circle the word that doesn't belong.

1. jugs   jars   pottery   monuments

2. festivals   marble   celebrations   drama

3. pottery   gods   buildings   monuments

4. sculptures   stone   drama   marble

5. drama   pottery   plays   amphitheater

Content Reading Strategy: Visualize

A. In Unit 1 you learned about the Egyptians. Visualize what you remember about the Egyptians. Then draw a picture below. Use the words in the box to help you visualize.

pyramid   mummy   pharaoh   hieroglyphics

B. Write a few sentences about your picture.

_____

_____

_____

_____

_____

_____

Unit 2: Lesson 1

Before You Read

Using Visuals: Use a Map Key

Look at the map and map key from page 40 in your Student Book. Then answer the questions.

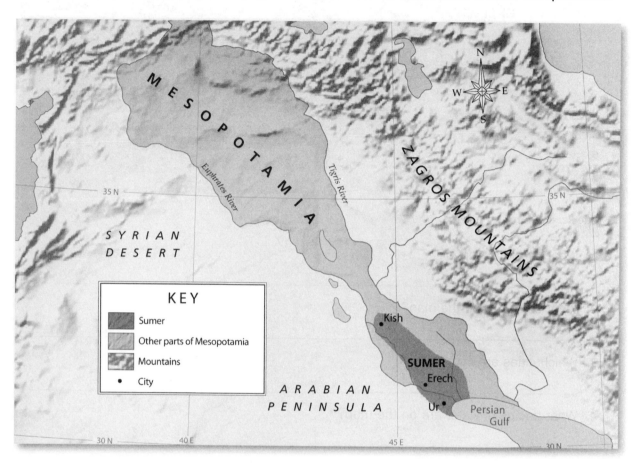

1. What large region is shown on the map?

   _____

2. Where is Sumer located?

   _____

3. What is the name of the mountain range?

   _____

4. What are the names of the cities?

   _____

5. Where are the cities located?

   _____

Using Visuals: Use a Map Key

Look at this map from page 56 in your Student Book. Then answer the questions.

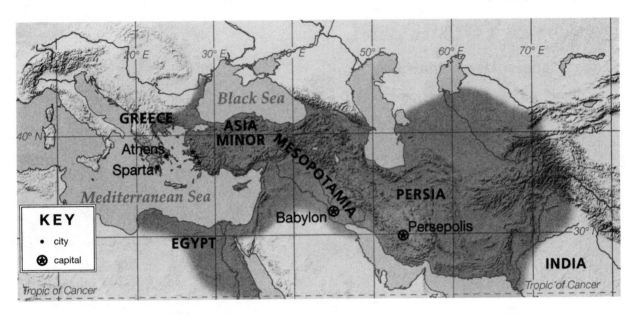

▲ The Persian Empire

1. What is this a map of?

   _____

2. What cities are on the map?

   _____

3. Which cities are capitals?

   _____

4. What bodies of water are on the map?

   _____

5. What symbol could you add to the map key?

   _____

Unit 2: Lesson 1

More Review and Practice

VOCABULARY

Complete the puzzle. Use key words.

ACROSS

1. an outdoor theater

2. structures built to honor gods

3. figures made of marble

DOWN

4. celebrations

5. a play acted in a theater

6. everyday objects made from clay

VOCABULARY IN CONTEXT

Complete the paragraph. Use words from the box.

| festivals | sculptures | drama | pottery | amphitheaters |

Greeks were skilled artists. They made **(1)** _____ from marble and stone. They also made decorative **(2)** _____ from clay.

(3) _____ was important to the Greeks. They performed plays at

(4) _____, or celebrations. Greeks built **(5)** _____ where people could sit to watch the plays.

TIMELINE CHECK

Use the timelines on pages 70–77 in your Student Book to answer the questions.

1. What happened in 432 B.C.E.? _____

2. When did Hippocrates found the science of medicine? _____

3. When did the Chinese begin to use a crossbow? _____

4. What did Alexander do in 327 B.C.E.? _____

_____

Choose the best answer. Circle the letter.

1. Pericles was a _____ in Athens.

   a. slave   **b.** leader   **c.** pharaoh

2. Greeks created the idea of _____.

   a. pharaohs   **b.** war   **c.** democracy

3. Sparta and Athens were _____.

   a. Greek festivals   **b.** independent city-states   **c.** Olympic games

4. Alexander the Great established many new _____ during his rule.

   a. amphitheaters   **b.** schools   **c.** cities

5. Spartan children studied _____.

   a. war   **b.** medicine   **c.** philosophy

APPLY SOCIAL STUDIES SKILLS

Content Reading Strategy: Visualize

Read this paragraph about homes in ancient Greece. Visualize a picture in your mind. Draw your picture in your notebook. Explain your picture to a classmate.

> Greek homes were made of mud bricks. There were two or three rooms around an open courtyard that was protected from the street. Larger homes had a kitchen, a storeroom, a room for bathing, a men's dining room, and a women's sitting area.

Using Visuals: Use a Map Key

Look at the map key below. Write what these symbols represent on a map.

Map Key	
✪	1. _____
•	2. _____
▲	3. _____
▬	4. _____

Unit 2: Lesson 2

Before You Read

VOCABULARY

A. Circle the best word to complete each sentence.

1. Romans who did not follow the laws went to a (senate / prison).

2. The (senate / Colosseum) was part of the Roman government. It helped make laws.

3. The (Colosseum / government) was an amphitheater for gladiator shows.

4. The Romans used (governments / aqueducts) to carry water to the city.

5. Monuments and buildings are examples of (structures / aqueducts).

6. The Roman (government / prison) was called a republic.

B. Draw an arrow between words that are related. Write four sentences to tell how they are related.

senate	punishment
prison	water
Colosseum	laws
aqueduct	gladiators

1. _____

2. _____

3. _____

4. _____

C. Write T for *true* or F for *false*.

_____ **1.** Romans built the Colosseum to carry water.

_____ **2.** The Roman senate made laws and advised the rulers.

_____ **3.** People who broke laws in Rome went to prison.

_____ **4.** The aqueducts held 45,000 people.

_____ **5.** The Roman government was a structure.

Content Reading Strategy: Ask Questions

A. Look at the picture. What questions do you have <u>before</u> you read the paragraph below? Write your questions next to the picture.

B. Read the paragraph about Roman prisons. What questions do you have <u>while</u> you read? Write your questions next to the paragraph.

     Roman prisons were dark, dirty, and smelly. People were sent there to wait for a punishment, usually death. There were narrow stairs, a small room, and a hole in the floor. The hole in the floor led to the dungeon, the room where the prisoners stayed.

     Rich people did not go to prison. Instead, they stayed under house arrest in their own homes.

C. What questions do you have <u>after</u> you finished reading? Write your questions here.

D. Now share your questions with a classmate. Does your classmate have similar questions?

Unit 2: Lesson 2

Before You Read

SOCIAL STUDIES SKILLS

Using Visuals: Use a Compass Rose

Look at this map of ancient Greece from page 69 in your Student Book. Find the compass rose on the map. Then answer the questions.

1. What cities are north of Sparta?

   _____

2. What mountain is south of Macedonia?

   _____

3. What sea is east of Greece?

   _____

4. Is Greece west or east of Asia Minor?

   _____

5. What island is southeast of Sparta?

   _____

Using Visuals: Use a Compass Rose

Look at this map of the empire of Alexander the Great from page 79 in your Student Book. Find the compass rose on the map. Then answer the questions.

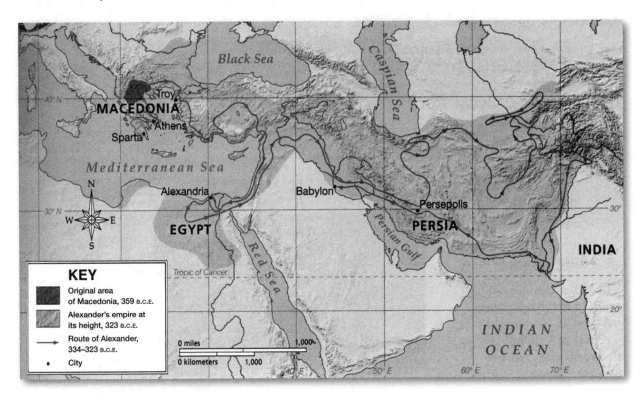

1. Which sea is directly north of Egypt?

   _____

2. Which cities are east of Alexandria?

   _____

3. Which cities are north of Alexandria?

   _____

4. Is Persia west of India?

   _____

5. Is Babylon east of Persepolis?

   _____

Unit 2: Lesson 2

More Review and Practice

VOCABULARY

Match the parts of the sentence. Write the letter.

_____ 1. The Colosseum

_____ 2. Romans who disobeyed laws

_____ 3. The first Roman government

_____ 4. Ancient structures

_____ 5. The Senate

_____ 6. The aqueducts of Rome

a. such as amphitheaters and aqueducts are still standing today.

b. was called a republic.

c. brought fresh water from the mountains.

d. was part of the Roman government.

e. was a famous structure used for entertainment.

f. went to prison.

VOCABULARY IN CONTEXT

Write T for *true* or F for *false.*

_____ 1. The poor people in Roman society received handouts from the prison.

_____ 2. The gladiators fought wild animals in the Colosseum.

_____ 3. The Roman senate was a powerful group in the government.

_____ 4. Bridges and buildings are aqueducts.

_____ 5. The Muslims conquered many structures.

TIMELINE CHECK

Use the timelines on pages 84–91 in your Student Book to answer the questions.

1. When was copper first used in East Africa?

_____

2. What happened in 14 c.e.?

_____

3. When did Mayan city-states flourish?

_____

4. What happened in 632 c.e.?

_____

Choose the best answer. Circle the letter.

1. Muslim _____ studied literature, science, and history.

   a. soldiers   **b.** scholars   **c.** senators

2. Constantinople and Baghdad were both _____.

   a. structures   **b.** rivers   **c.** centers of trade

3. A group of senators _____ Julius Caesar.

   a. assassinated   **b.** ruled   **c.** studied

4. Justinian's Code was a _____.

   a. system of trade   **b.** new form of literature   **c.** system of laws

5. _____ is one reason the Roman Empire began to decline.

   a. Lack of water   **b.** Corrupt emperors   **c.** War with Greece

APPLY SOCIAL STUDIES SKILLS

Content Reading Strategy: Ask Questions

Read the paragraph below about an ancient structure. Ask yourself questions before, during, and after you read. Write the questions on the right.

Emperor Constantine built a horse-racing track called the Hippodrome. It was in the capital city of Constantinople. The Hippodrome was very large and beautiful. It was the center of social activity. People came to see the chariot races. It had space for 100,000 people. Today only a few columns of the original structure remain in a park in Istanbul, Turkey.

Questions before Reading
Questions while Reading
Questions after Reading

Using Visuals: Use a Compass Rose

Use the map of Constantinople on page 93 in your Student Book to answer T for *true* or F for *false.*

_____ **1.** The Golden Horn is northeast of the city.

_____ **2.** Cisterns, large containers for water, are south of Forum Bovi.

_____ **3.** The aqueduct is east of the palace.

_____ **4.** The Hippodrome is southeast of the Forum of Constantine.

_____ **5.** The Wall of Constantine is east of most structures in the city.

Unit 2

Unit Review

VOCABULARY

Choose a word from the box to replace the words in *italics*. Write that word on the line.

drama	pottery	Colosseum	aqueducts	amphitheater
senate	festivals	sculptures	prison	structures

1. Emperor Vespasian built the *large amphitheater* in Rome. _____

2. The ancient Greeks made *everyday objects from clay.* _____

3. The Romans built many *buildings and aqueducts.* _____

4. The ancient Greeks held *celebrations* such as the Olympic Games. _____

5. The Romans built *large structures to carry water.* _____

6. The *group of men who made the laws* in Rome had some very great speakers.

_____

7. Plays were performed for audiences in an *outdoor theater.* _____

8. *Figures made from marble* decorated Greek buildings. _____

9. Romans who did not obey the laws went to a *place to hold people.* _____

10. The ancient Greeks performed *plays* at festivals. _____

VOCABULARY IN CONTEXT

Complete each sentence. Use words from the box. There is one extra word.

monument	government	prison	sculptures	drama	pottery

1. The archaeologist found a very old piece of clay _____.

2. A pyramid is a _____ in Egypt.

3. There are many marble _____ at the art museum.

4. We still punish people today by sending them to a _____.

5. The _____ of Rome began as a republic.

Put the events in the correct order. Number them from 1 to 6.

_____ Justinian began to rule the Byzantine Empire.

_____ Alexander became king.

_____ Cleopatra became the queen of Egypt.

_____ Roman emperor Augustus died.

_____ The Golden Age of the Muslim Empire began.

_____ Sparta won the Peloponnesian War against Athens.

APPLY SOCIAL STUDIES SKILLS

Using Visuals: Use a Map Key and Compass Rose

Look at the map of the Byzantine Empire and Islamic world on page 91 in your Student Book. Find the map key and compass rose on the map. Then answer the questions.

1. What dates does the map key include?

_____

2. Is the area of the Roman Empire from an earlier time?

_____

3. What does the red line show?

_____

4. What city is farthest north on the map?

_____

5. What city is farthest south on the map?

_____

EXTENSION PROJECT

Many people today visit ancient monuments. Choose one country (Egypt, Greece, Turkey, or Italy) and make a map of the locations of some ancient structures that are still standing.

Unit 2

Writing Skills

WRITE A PARAGRAPH

A. Read the following paragraph. Then circle the best topic sentence for this paragraph.

Poor Romans were either slaves or men with no jobs. The men without jobs had to live by getting help from the government to feed their families. The slaves worked in rich people's houses or on farms. The rich had beautiful homes and plenty of food to eat.

Possible Topic Sentences

- Rich Romans ate large meals called feasts.

- Poor Roman people lived in bad housing.

- The lives of rich and poor people in Rome were very different.

B. Read another paragraph. Then circle the best topic sentence for this paragraph.

The ancient Greeks and Romans loved to watch chariot races. A man drove two or four horses standing in a wagon, or chariot. The chariots and horses went very fast around the ring. It took great skill to drive the horses so fast. Big crowds of people, sometimes 250,000, came to see the chariot races. The racers were divided into teams by colors: red, white, blue, and green. People bet money on the races.

Possible Topic Sentences

- The ruler dropped a white cloth to start the race.

- Chariot races were a popular form of entertainment in Greece and Rome.

- People dressed in their best clothes to go to the chariot races.

C. Read the following paragraph. Change the first sentence to a strong topic sentence for this paragraph.

Boys in Sparta received training. Spartan boys began training at seven years old. They went to live in a camp with other boys and learned how to use swords and spears. It was a very hard life. They were not given comfortable beds or much food to eat. This was to prepare them for life as a soldier.

D. Now write your own paragraph. Choose one of the topics in the box. Begin with a topic sentence. Use your own words. Have a classmate check your paragraph.

Athens	Byzantium	Macedonia
Baghdad	Constantinople	Rome

Unit 3: Lesson 1

Before You Read

VOCABULARY

A. Match the key words with a definition. Write the letter.

_____ **1.** crusade   **a.** people who worked and lived on a manor

_____ **2.** peasants   **b.** a soldier for a lord or king

_____ **3.** manor   **c.** a Christian war against the Muslims

_____ **4.** feudalism   **d.** a large village owned by a lord

_____ **5.** cathedral   **e.** a type of government based on a class system

_____ **6.** knight   **f.** a very large church

B. Write four sentences using a key word and its definition.

  1. _____

  2. _____

  3. _____

  4. _____

C. Complete each sentence. Use words from the box.

feudalism   cathedrals   crusade   peasant   knight   manor

  1. A _____ was a soldier for a lord or king.

  2. Knights went to fight in a _____.

  3. Peasants and lords lived on a _____.

  4. The Roman Catholic Church built _____.

  5. A _____ worked for the lord of the manor.

  6. _____ was a form of government based on a class system.

D. Circle the word that doesn't belong.

  1. armor   horse   farmer   knight

  2. feudalism   lord   cathedral   peasant

  3. crusade   soldier   war   manor

  4. cathedral   armor   church   Roman Catholic

Content Reading Strategy: Monitor Comprehension

Look at the picture. Read the paragraph. As you read, check your understanding about knights. Then answer the questions.

A Knight's Armor

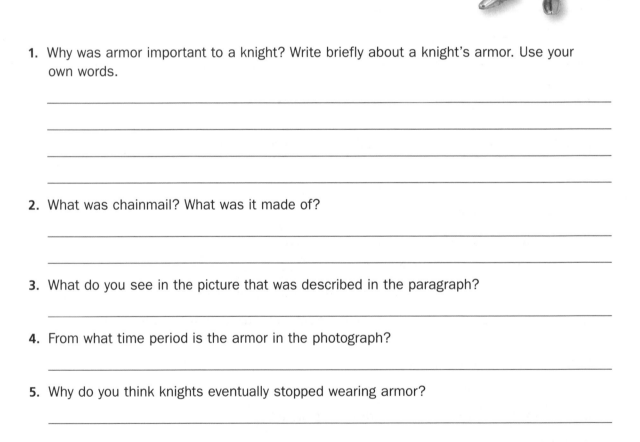

Armor was very important to a knight. It protected him in battle. A knight's armor consisted of hard plates and chainmail. Hard plates of metal protected sensitive areas, such as the chest, back, and shoulders. Chainmail, made of tiny rings of metal attached tightly together, was worn on all the other areas. The knight wore a metal helmet. Even the knight's horse wore armor. Later, in the fifteenth century, knights began to wear full-body metal armor, and chainmail was no longer used.

1. Why was armor important to a knight? Write briefly about a knight's armor. Use your own words.

   _____

   _____

   _____

   _____

2. What was chainmail? What was it made of?

   _____

   _____

3. What do you see in the picture that was described in the paragraph?

   _____

4. From what time period is the armor in the photograph?

   _____

5. Why do you think knights eventually stopped wearing armor?

   _____

Unit 3: Lesson 1

Before You Read

Content Reading Strategy: Monitor Comprehension

Look at the picture. Read the paragraph. As you read, check your understanding about the Middle Ages. Then answer the questions.

The Ruling Class in the Middle Ages

Kings, lords, and knights were the ruling class. The king ruled over large areas of land. To protect his land, the king gave some land to lords. The lords in return promised to protect the king and the land. The knights worked for the lords and the king. They were soldiers who promised to fight in return for land that the lord gave them. The ruling class called themselves noblemen. Noblewomen were the wives and daughters of kings, lords, and knights. When a nobleman was away, his wife was in charge of the manor.

1. Who was part of the ruling class? Write briefly about the ruling class. Use your own words.

   _____

   _____

   _____

2. What do you see in the picture?

   _____

3. Who were the noblewomen?

   _____

Using Visuals: Read a Map

Look at the map of Europe in 1400. Then answer the questions about latitude and longitude.

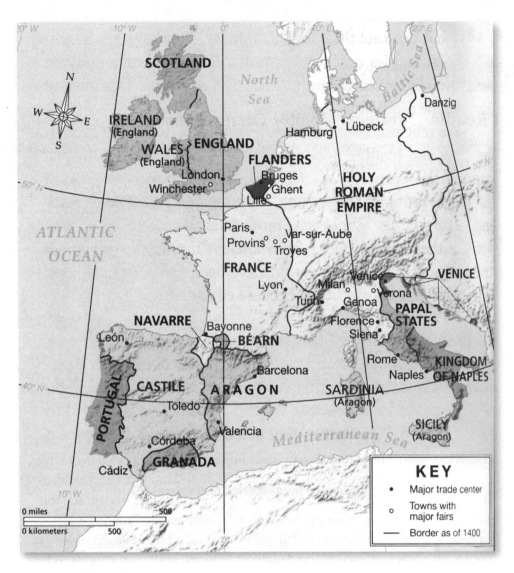

1. In which direction do the lines of latitude go on the map?

_____

2. In which direction do the lines of longitude go on the map?

_____

3. What line of latitude goes through Castile and Aragon?

_____

4. What city is located on 2°E longitude and 48°N latitude?

_____

5. What lines of longitude and latitude go through the Holy Roman Empire?

_____

Unit 3: Lesson 1

More Review and Practice

VOCABULARY

Match the parts of the sentence. Write the letter.

_____ **1.** The peasants   **a.** was a type of government.

_____ **2.** A cathedral   **b.** was a soldier.

_____ **3.** A manor   **c.** were the poorest people on a manor.

_____ **4.** A knight   **d.** was a large village with farms and pastures.

_____ **5.** Feudalism   **e.** had large windows made of colored glass.

VOCABULARY IN CONTEXT

Complete the paragraph. Use words from the box. There is one extra word.

knight	Crusades	cathedral	feudalism	manor	peasants

The system of government in Europe during the Middle Ages was called

(1) _____. It divided society into two classes: the ruling class and

the working class. A **(2)** _____ was a soldier who belonged to the

ruling class. He fought in the **(3)** _____ for the Church. He also fought

to protect his lord. **(4)** _____ belonged to the working class. The rich

and the poor lived on a **(5)** _____, but in separate areas.

TIMELINE CHECK

Use the timelines on pages 104–111 in your Student Book to answer the questions.

1. What event happened in 1099?

_____

2. When did the Turks defeat the Byzantine emperor Romanus IV? _____

3. Did Charlemagne die before or after the Holy Roman Empire was divided?

_____

4. What did the Mongols under Genghis Khan do in 1215?

_____

5. When was Muhammad born? _____

Choose the best answer. Circle the letter.

1. The religion of Islam comes from _____.

   a. Justinian's Code   b. Muhammad's teachings   c. the pope's teachings

2. The period of the Middle Ages was from about _____.

   a. 500 to 1500   b. 1000 to 2000   c. 200 to 1000

3. _____ opened new trade routes and brought new knowledge to Europe.

   a. The manor system   b. The Crusaders   c. The peasants

4. Cities developed _____ in the 1300s.

   a. very slowly   b. into manors   c. very quickly

5. Charlemagne _____ Europe for the first time since the Roman Empire.

   a. united   b. divided   c. fought

APPLY SOCIAL STUDIES SKILLS

Content Reading Strategy: Monitor Comprehension

Read the paragraph. As you read, check your understanding about the manor and peasants. Then answer the questions.

> The local lord or vassal ruled the peasants. The peasants produced everything that the manor needed. Peasant men, women, and children worked in the fields, took care of the animals, built and took care of all the structures on the manor, made the clothing, and cut the wood. Peasants had a very small piece of land for themselves, but they had to pay taxes to the lord and give him part of their harvest.

1. What did you learn about peasants from the paragraph?

   _____

   _____

   _____

2. Why were peasants poor?

   _____

Using Visuals: Read a Map

Look at the map on page 113 in your Student Book. Write the approximate longitude and latitude of the following cities.

1. Marseille _____   2. Metz _____   3. Edessa _____

Unit 3: Lesson 2

Before You Read

VOCABULARY

A. Complete the puzzle. Use key words.

ACROSS

1. people who lived under cliffs

2. a Japanese warrior

3. material made from silkworm fibers

DOWN

4. different emperors from the same family

5. buy and sell goods

6. a waterway

B. Draw an arrow between words that are related. Write four sentences to tell how they are related.

dynasty	canals	samurai	trade
cliff dwellers	silk	China	warrior

1. _____

2. _____

3. _____

4. _____

C. Write T for *true* or F for *false.* Correct the sentences that are false.

_____ **1.** Dynasties ruled in Europe.

_____ **2.** A samurai warrior was trained not to show fear.

_____ **3.** Cliff dwellers were a group of people who lived on canals.

_____ **4.** Silk is a soft fiber made from the thread of silkworms.

_____ **5.** The Church traded silk with other parts of the world.

Content Reading Strategy: Understand Chronological Order

A. Read the following paragraph about the Kingdom of Ghana. Underline words and dates that help you understand the chronological order.

> The Kingdom of Ghana was the first West African kingdom to become rich from trading salt and gold. By 400 the Ghanaian empire controlled all the trade routes across the Sahara Desert. By 800 Ghana had reached its height as a major trading kingdom. Later, a Muslim group called the Almoravids began to battle with the people of Ghana. It was a long struggle, but finally the Almoravids conquered the area and took the gold. By 1100 the Kingdom of Ghana was very weak. Another group, the Soso people, took over the area.

B. Make a timeline below using your underlined words and dates.

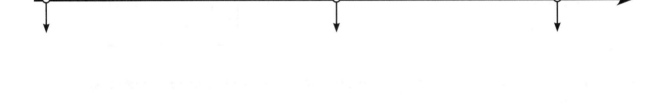

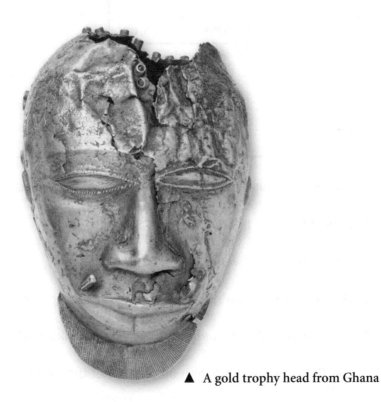

▲ A gold trophy head from Ghana

Unit 3: Lesson 2

Before You Read

Content Reading Strategy: Understand Chronological Order

A. Read the following paragraph about two Mongol leaders. Underline words and dates that help you understand the chronological order.

Genghis Khan was one of the most well known conquerors in the world. He was born around 1167 in what is now eastern Mongolia. In 1206 he became the first great khan of the Mongol Empire. In 1207 Genghis Khan led the Mongols on the first of many bloody invasions. After many military successes, he died in 1227. Later, in 1260, Genghis Khan's grandson, Kublai Khan, became the ruler of the Mongol Empire. Kublai Khan allowed religious freedom and made many improvements in his empire. When he died in 1294, the Mongols became less warlike.

B. Make a timeline below using your underlined words and dates.

Using Visuals: Use a Map Scale

Look at the map of Asian civilizations from page 117 in your Student Book. Use the map scale to answer the questions.

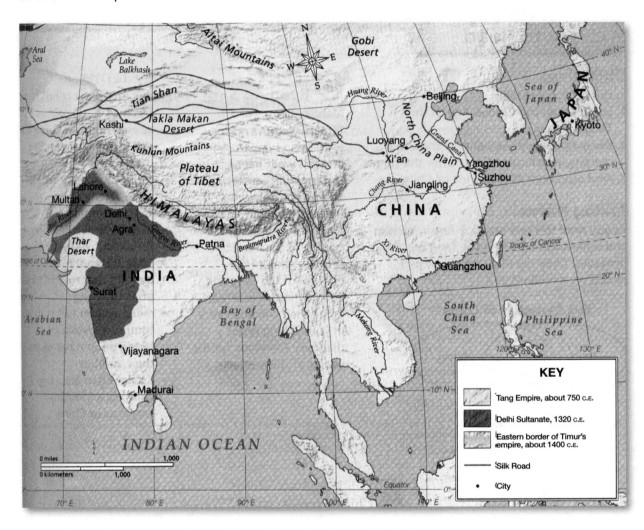

1. About how many miles is it from Surat to Madurai in India?

   _____

2. How many miles across is the Bay of Bengal at its widest part?

   _____

3. About how many miles is it from Xi'an to Yangzhou?

   _____

4. About how many miles is it from Patna to Guangzhou?

   _____

5. Which is longer, a kilometer or a mile?

   _____

Unit 3: Lesson 2

More Review and Practice

VOCABULARY

Complete the puzzle. Use key words. Write the secret word.

1. a group of people who lived under cliffs
   ◯ __ __ __ __ __ __ __ __ __ __ __

2. buying, exchanging, or selling goods
   __ __ ◯ __ __

3. a family of rulers
   __ __ ◯ __ __ __ __

4. a Japanese warrior
   __ __ __ __ __ ◯ __

5. material made from soft fiber
   __ __ ◯ __

Secret word: __ __ __ __ __

VOCABULARY IN CONTEXT

Write T for *true* or F for *false*. Correct the sentences that are false.

_____ **1.** The Song dynasty was a government in Japan.

_____ **2.** The Chinese government built a 1,000-mile-long canal.

_____ **3.** The civilizations in Mesoamerica had samurai warriors.

_____ **4.** The Silk Road was a place where ships passed through.

_____ **5.** Trade increased while Kublai Khan was Emperor of China.

TIMELINE CHECK

Use the timelines on pages 118–125 in your Student Book to answer the questions.

1. When did the Black Death kill millions of people? _____

2. Was the city of Delhi founded in India before or after the Huns invaded? _____

   _____

3. When did the Aztecs begin living in Tenochtitlán?_____

   _____

4. What happened in 1192? _____

5. What happened in 1294? _____

Choose the best answer. Circle the letter.

1. One great civilization in Mesoamerica was _____.

   a. the Mayan civilization   **b.** the Tang dynasty   **c.** the cliff dwellers

2. The Aztecs built _____.

   a. mounds   **b.** Tenochtitlán   **c.** a 1,000-mile canal

3. _____ valued art, books, and beautiful objects.

   a. The Mongols   **b.** The Song dynasty   **c.** The Anasazi

4. Japan had a _____ system in the eleventh century.

   a. nomadic   **b.** foreign   **c.** feudal

5. The Mongols were _____.

   a. horsemen and warriors   **b.** farmers and peasants   **c.** cliff dwellers and hunters

APPLY SOCIAL STUDIES SKILLS

Content Reading Strategy: Understand Chronological Order

Read the paragraph. Underline the dates and important events. List them below in chronological order.

There were many great civilizations in Mesoamerica. The Mayas lived in Mesoamerica beginning around 250. They abandoned their cities around 900. The Aztecs lived in the area of present-day Mexico from the 1100s. By the 1470s they had spread to surrounding areas. The Aztecs ruled until the Spanish invaded in 1519.

Date   **Event**

Using Visuals: Use a Map Scale

Use the map of Japan on page 122 in your Student Book to answer T for *true* or F for *false*.

_____ **1.** It is about 250 miles from Kyoto to Tokyo.

_____ **2.** It is about 500 miles across the Korea Strait from Korea to Kyūshū.

_____ **3.** It is about 150 miles from the closest part of China to Korea.

_____ **4.** It is about 1,000 miles from Tokyo to the island of Hokkaidō.

Unit 3

Unit Review

VOCABULARY

Circle the best word to complete each sentence.

1. The Chinese and the cliff dwellers built (cathedrals / canals).

2. Under the shogun system, a (samurai / knight) fought for his warlord.

3. Serfs lived on a (manor / canal) and worked in the fields.

4. The Chinese traded porcelain and (books / silk) to middlemen.

5. The Roman Catholic Church organized the (dynasties / Crusades).

6. (Feudalism / Religion) was a system of government in Europe and Japan.

7. The Anasazi were (cliff dwellers / nomads) who lived in North America.

8. Many (cathedrals / manors) in Europe had stained glass windows.

9. (War / Trade) increased between Europe and China after Marco Polo visited Kublai Khan.

10. A (dynasty / samurai) is a series of rulers from the same family.

VOCABULARY IN CONTEXT

Complete the paragraph. Use words from the box. There is one extra word.

crusade	samurai	knights	manor	feudalism	peasants

    Japan and Europe both had a system of **(1)** _____ during the Middle

Ages. **(2)** _____ worked the land for nobles. In Europe, many people lived

on a **(3)** _____. Nobles hired **(4)** _____ to protect their

land and fight for them. In Japan, the nobles hired **(5)** _____ warriors

for the same reason.

Match the events with the dates on the timeline. Write the date next to the event.

618   1100   1348 1368

_____ The Black Death sweeps across Europe.   _____ The Tang dynasty starts.

_____ Aztecs begin living in Tenochtitlán.   _____ Mongols overthrown in China.

APPLY SOCIAL STUDIES SKILLS

Using Visuals: Read a Map and Use a Map Scale

Look at the map from page 127 in your Student Book. Then answer the questions.

1. What city is near 70°W and 15°S? _____

2. Is Middle America north or south the equator? _____

3. What degrees of longitude is the Gulf of Mexico between? _____

4. About how many miles is it across the middle of North America? _____

5. How many miles is it from the equator to the Tropic of Capricorn? _____

EXTENSION PROJECT

Research one early invention of the Chinese such as gunpowder, fireworks, ink, the compass, or the printing press. Look on the Internet and in reference books. Write a paragraph about it.

Unit 3

Writing Skills

MAKE AN OUTLINE

A. Read the following paragraph. Then complete the outline to highlight the important information.

During feudal times, Japanese society was ruled by a class system. The emperor and shogun were the main rulers. The emperor was the head of the government. He appointed a shogun. He gave the shogun power to make laws, collect taxes, and protect the land from foreign invaders. Shoguns protected the land through their warlords.

Warlords and samurai warriors formed clans to protect the shogun. The warlords controlled large armies. Samurai warriors were special soldiers with martial arts training. They followed the orders of their warlords. The samurai swore to die for the warlords.

I.   The class system of Japan during feudalism

   A. The emperor and the shogun ruled Japan.

     1.

     2.

     3.

   B. Warlords and samurai warriors formed clans to protect the shogun.

     1.

     2.

     3.

B. Choose a topic from the list of Unit Contents on page 99 in your Student Book. Gather information. Make an outline. Then write a paragraph from your outline.

Outline

    I.

       A.

          1.

          2.

          3.

       B.

          1.

          2.

          3.

Paragraph

Unit 4: Lesson 1

Before You Read

VOCABULARY

A. Match the key words with a definition. Write the letter.

_____ **1.** clergy   **a.** public complaints

_____ **2.** explorer   **b.** a book written by hand

_____ **3.** printing press   **c.** leaders of a church

_____ **4.** movable type   **d.** a person who looks for new territory

_____ **5.** manuscript   **e.** small metal letters used in printing

_____ **6.** protests   **f.** an invention for making books and newspapers

B. Write four sentences using a key word and its definition.

1. _____

2. _____

3. _____

4. _____

C. Complete each sentence. Use words from the box.

clergy   protests   explorer   manuscript   printing press   movable type

1. Before the _____, books were written by hand.

2. A book written by hand is a _____.

3. The use of _____ helped to produce books more quickly.

4. The Jesuits were a group of _____.

5. Fernando Magellan was an _____.

6. Martin Luther made a list of _____ against the Roman Catholic Church.

D. Circle the word that doesn't belong.

1. clergy   Jesuits   printing press   church

2. explorer   Magellan   ships   protests

3. protests   soldier   complaints   Luther

4. printing press   movable type   explorer   manuscript

Content Reading Strategy: Reread

A. Read the paragraph. Then write what you think the main idea is.

> Ferdinand Magellan was a sea explorer. He was born in Portugal. He was the first explorer to sail west from Europe to Asia. He was the first European to sail in the Pacific Ocean. The Strait of Magellan in South America was named in his honor. A strait is a narrow waterway. Magellan found an animal in South America called the llama. This animal was unknown to the Europeans.

Main idea:

_____

B. Reread the paragraph for details. Answer the questions.

1. Who was Ferdinand Magellan?

_____

2. Where was Ferdinand Magellan from?

_____

3. Where did Ferdinand Magellan sail?

_____

4. What is a strait?

_____

5. What animal did Ferdinand Magellan find in South America?

_____

Unit 4: Lesson 1

Before You Read

SOCIAL STUDIES SKILLS

Content Reading Strategy: Reread

A. Read the paragraph. Then write what you think the main idea is.

> The city of Jerusalem has a very long history of conflict. The first Crusaders marched from Europe to Jerusalem in 1099 to battle the Muslims. The Christians took over the city and Jerusalem became the capital of the Kingdom of Jerusalem, a feudal state. Neither Jews nor Muslims were allowed to live in the city. In 1187 a Muslim leader named Salah al-Din took Jerusalem back from the Crusaders and opened the city to all religious groups. In 1243 Jerusalem came under the control of the Christians again for a short time. But in 1244 the Muslims took the city back, only to be driven out by the Egyptians in 1247. Finally, in 1517, the Ottoman Empire took control of Jerusalem and people enjoyed religious harmony until the mid-nineteenth century.

Main idea:

_____

B. Reread the paragraph for details. Answer the questions.

1. What groups fought to control Jerusalem?

_____

2. When did the first Crusade take control of Jerusalem?

_____

3. Who conquered Jerusalem in 1187?

_____

4. What happened in 1247?

_____

5. How long did the city of Jerusalem enjoy religious harmony under the Ottoman Empire?

_____

Using Visuals: Use Physical Maps

Look at the physical map of Europe from page 137 in your Student Book. Then answer the questions.

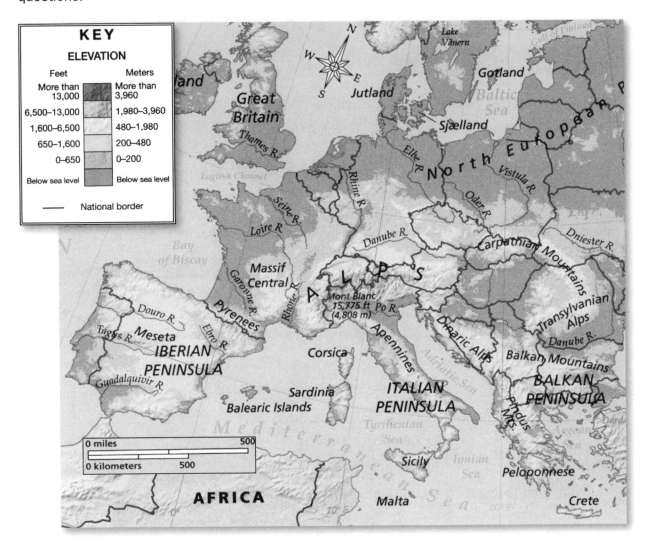

1. What continent is south of Europe?

_____

2. What mountain ranges are north of the Balkan Peninsula?

_____

3. Is the English Channel to the north or south of Great Britain?

_____

4. What islands are to the west of the Italian Peninsula?

_____

5. Is the Danube River in eastern, central, or western Europe?

_____

Unit 4: Lesson 1
More Review and Practice

VOCABULARY

Match the parts of the sentence. Write the letter.

_____ **1.** A manuscript

_____ **2.** The Roman Catholic Church

_____ **3.** An explorer

_____ **4.** Martin Luther

_____ **5.** Movable type

_____ **6.** The printing press

a. was small metal letters used for printing.

b. sailed to unknown lands.

c. made producing books much easier.

d. was a book or document written by hand.

e. nailed a list of protests on a church door.

f. created a group of clergy called Jesuits.

VOCABULARY IN CONTEXT

Complete the paragraph. Use words from the box. There is one extra word.

protests	clergy	manuscripts	printing press	movable type

Johannes Gutenberg invented the **(1)** _____ and

(2) _____. These inventions made books much quicker and easier to

produce. Before these inventions, people wrote **(3)** _____. Martin Luther

wrote his list of **(4)** _____ by hand.

TIMELINE CHECK

Use the timelines on pages 138–145 in your Student Book to answer the questions.

1. When was Leonardo da Vinci born?_____

2. What happened in 1385? _____

_____

3. When did the Muslims recapture Jerusalem? _____

4. Which happened first—a peasant revolt in Germany or a peasant revolt in China?

_____

5. When did Martin Luther nail his list of protests onto a church door?

_____

Choose the best answer. Circle the letter.

1. Johannes Gutenberg invented _____ around 1455.

   a. the Bible   **b.** the telescope   **c.** the printing press

2. Traders used the Silk Road to _____.

   a. exchange goods   **b.** build the Great Wall   **c.** find gold and silver

3. The Renaissance lasted from _____.

   a. the 1600s to the 1900s   **b.** the 1700s to the 1800s   **c.** the 1300s to the 1600s

4. Martin Luther's protests eventually forced the Roman Catholic Church to _____.

   a. invent the printing press   **b.** make changes   **c.** read more books

5. The Renaissance was _____.

   a. a protest against the Church   **b.** a period of cultural change   **c.** a new invention

APPLY SOCIAL STUDIES SKILLS

Content Reading Strategy: Reread

Reread the paragraph about Lutheranism on page 145 in your Student Book. Then answer the questions.

1. How did the Roman Catholic Church feel about Martin Luther?

   _____

2. What did the Roman Catholic Church eventually do?

   _____

Using Visuals: Physical Maps

Look at the map of Italy on page 147 in your Student Book to answer the questions.

1. What were the names of the states in northern Italy?

   _____

2. What two islands are west of Naples?

   _____

3. Where is Sicily located on the map?

   _____

4. Is Italy an island or a peninsula?

   _____

Unit 4: Lesson 2

Before You Read

VOCABULARY

A. Match the key words with a definition. Write the letter.

_____ **1.** route	**a.**	originally in a place
_____ **2.** diseases	**b.**	taken by force
_____ **3.** indigenous	**c.**	illnesses
_____ **4.** navigation	**d.**	trips on the ocean
_____ **5.** conquered	**e.**	the science of finding your way on the ocean
_____ **6.** voyages	**f.**	the path or way to another place

B. Write four sentences using a key word and its definition.

1. _____

2. _____

3. _____

4. _____

C. Write T for *true* or F for *false*. Correct the sentences that are false.

_____ **1.** Voyages were trips made on a horse.

_____ **2.** The Aztecs were one group of indigenous people.

_____ **3.** The Portuguese used a compass for navigation.

_____ **4.** The explorers conquered many routes.

_____ **5.** The Americas brought diseases to the indigenous people.

D. Circle the word that doesn't belong.

1. route	way	Aztecs	exploration
2. navigation	ocean	compass	smallpox
3. indigenous	compass	Aztecs	Americas
4. smallpox	route	voyage	travel
5. smallpox	Atlantic	diseases	death

Content Reading Strategy: Use Selective Attention

A. Think about this question before you read the paragraph: *What was important about the Renaissance?* Use selective attention to find the answer. Write your answer below the paragraph.

   The Renaissance started in Italy. It was an important period of scientific discoveries and artistic changes. Leonardo da Vinci was one of the great painters of the Renaissance. He painted the *Mona Lisa.* Michelangelo painted the ceiling of the Sistine Chapel. Later the Renaissance spread to Germany. In the 1450s a German printer named Johannes Gutenberg invented movable type and a printing press.

_____

_____

B. Reread the paragraph. Use selective attention to find information to write in the chart below.

Name	Artist or Inventor?	Painting or Invention?

C. Think about how you used selective attention. Then answer the questions.

   1. What clues helped you find the answer to the question in A. above?

_____

   2. What strategy did you use to complete the chart?

_____

   3. How did you find the answers in the paragraph?

_____

Unit 4: Lesson 2

Before You Read

SOCIAL STUDIES SKILLS

Content Reading Strategy: Use Selective Attention

A. Think about this question before you read the paragraph: *What is the scientific method?* Use selective attention to find the answer. Write your answer below the paragraph.

During the 1600s, new scientific discoveries encouraged new ways of thinking. This period was the Age of Enlightenment. It started a scientific revolution. Scientists developed the scientific method, a way of performing experiments. Galileo Galilei used this method to prove that the sun was at the center of our solar system. Sir Isaac Newton also used the scientific method to explain how gravity controls the movement of the earth around the sun.

_____

_____

B. What steps did you follow to answer the question? Complete the sentences with words from the box.

answered	reread	read	words	sentences

1. First, I _____ the paragraph.

2. Second, I _____ the question.

3. Third, I looked for key _____ and _____.

4. Finally, I _____ the question.

C. Now use selective attention to answer the questions.

1. What was the Age of Enlightenment?

_____

2. What method did Galileo use to prove his theory?

_____

3. What theory did Sir Isaac Newton prove?

_____

Using Visuals: Use Different Types of Maps

Compare the maps below. Then answer the questions.

◀ Europe, 1500s

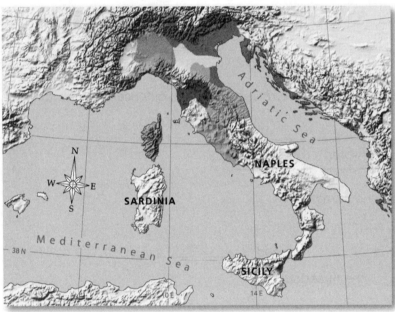

◀ Italy, 1510

1. Which map is a political map? Why?

_____

2. Which map is a physical map? Why?

_____

3. Which map shows country borders? _____

4. What region do these maps share? _____

5. Which map shows a larger area? _____

Unit 4: Lesson 2

More Review and Practice

VOCABULARY

Complete the puzzle. Use key words. Write the secret word.

1. Native peoples ⬭ __ __ __ __ __ __ __ __ __

2. Explorers use a compass to help with this. ⬭ __ __ __ __ __ __ __ __ __

3. The Europeans took over the land and people. ⬭ __ __ __ __ __ __ __ __

4. Illnesses that killed many Aztecs and Incas __ __ __ __ __ ⬭ __ __ __

5. Columbus made four of these trips to America. __ __ __ __ __ __ ⬭

Secret word: __ __ __ __ __

VOCABULARY IN CONTEXT

Write T for *true* or F for *false*. Correct the sentences that are false.

_____ 1. The Silk Road was a trade route.

_____ 2. The Aztecs sailed around the Cape of Good Hope.

_____ 3. Europeans brought many diseases to the Americas.

_____ 4. The Incas conquered the Spanish army.

_____ 5. Spanish explorers made many voyages to the Americas.

TIMELINE CHECK

Use the timelines on pages 152–159 in your Student Book to answer the questions.

1. What did Sir Isaac Newton do in 1682?

   _____

2. Did Francisco Pizarro kill the Incan emperor in 1533 or 1524? _____

3. When did Joan of Arc fight the Battle of Orléans?

   _____

4. What happened in 1507?

   _____

5. When did Hernán Cortés arrive in Mexico? _____

Choose the best answer. Circle the letter.

1. The Portuguese were the first Europeans to bring _____ to the Americas.

   a. Incas   **b.** Africans   **c.** Aztecs

2. _____ was the center of the Aztec Empire.

   a. Moctezuma   **b.** Cortés   **c.** Tenochtitlán

3. Galileo Galilei was the first person to use _____ to study the planets and stars.

   a. a compass   **b.** a telescope   **c.** gravity

4. The Roman Catholic Church _____ Galileo's ideas.

   a. disagreed with   **b.** agreed with   **c.** didn't care about

5. Cortés and Pizarro were Spanish _____.

   a. scientists   **b.** kings   **c.** explorers

APPLY SOCIAL STUDIES SKILLS

Content Reading Strategy: Use Selective Attention

Read the paragraph. Then answer this question: *Who lived in Mexico, the Incas or the Aztecs?*

> There were many great civilizations in Mesoamerica. The Aztecs lived in the area of present-day Mexico. They built Tenochtitlán. The Incas lived in present-day Peru. They built Machu Picchu. The Spanish conquered the Incas. The Europeans eventually conquered all the indigenous peoples of Mesoamerica.

What key words or sentences helped you answer the question?

_____

_____

Using Visuals: Use Different Types of Maps

Use the maps on page 151 in your Student Book to answer T for *true* or F for *false*.

_____ **1.** A physical map shows a country's capital.

_____ **2.** A physical map shows rivers and mountains.

_____ **3.** A political map shows cities and states.

_____ **4.** A physical map shows the height of land above sea level.

_____ **5.** A political map shows mountain ranges, elevations, and plains.

Unit 4

Unit Review

VOCABULARY

Circle the best word to complete each sentence.

1. The Aztecs and Incas were (Spanish / indigenous) people of the Americas.

2. Magellan was a European (explorer / Jesuit).

3. Merchants used trade (compasses / routes) to bring new products to Europe.

4. A (manuscript / route) is a handwritten document.

5. Hernán Cortés (conquered / traded) the Aztecs.

6. Martin Luther made a list of (protests / voyages) against the Roman Catholic Church.

7. (Movable type / Navigation) was invented by Gutenberg.

8. Explorers used the compass for (printing / navigation).

VOCABULARY IN CONTEXT

Complete the paragraph. Use words from the box. There is one extra word.

voyages	navigation	routes	explorers	clergy	conquered

European **(1)** _____ made many **(2)** _____ to the
Americas. They used a compass to help with the **(3)** _____ of their
ships. They opened new trade **(4)** _____. They traded with the indigenous
people. They eventually **(5)** _____ them.

TIMELINE CHECK

Match the events with the dates on the timeline. Write the date next to the event.

1452	1532	1632	1682

_____ **1.** Sir Isaac Newton discovers the law of universal gravitation.

_____ **2.** Galileo Galilei publishes *The Dialogue.*

_____ **3.** Francisco Pizarro travels to Cuzco.

_____ **4.** Leonardo da Vinci is born.

Using Visuals: Use Different Types Of Maps

Color and label the following key physical features of North America on the map below.

1. The Canadian Shield
2. The Great Plains
3. The Sierra Madre Occidental
4. The Rocky Mountains
5. The Appalachian Mountains

Look at the map on page 161 in your Student Book to help you.

EXTENSION PROJECT

Research one scientific discovery or invention from the Renaissance (1300s–1600s). Find out who made the discovery or invention. Write a paragraph about it.

Unit 4

Writing Skills

WRITE A FIRST DRAFT

A. Read the following outline. Then write a first draft paragraph from the outline.

Outline

   I.   The Spanish Empire wanted new colonies.

      A. The Spanish rulers paid for expeditions.

         1. They gave Columbus three ships.

         2. They asked him to find new land and a new trade route.

         3. He landed in the Bahamas in 1492.

         4. He claimed that land for Spain.

      B. Explorers received rewards for new territory.

         1. They received money.

         2. They received titles of nobility.

Paragraph

B. Choose a topic from the list of Unit Contents on page 133 in your Student Book. First, write an outline below. Then write a first draft paragraph. Remember to write in your own words. You can edit your first draft later.

Outline

I.

    A.

        1.

        2.

        3.

    B.

        1.

        2.

        3.

Paragraph

Unit 5: Lesson 1

Before You Read

VOCABULARY

A. Write the key words from the box under the correct category.

People	Places

| colony |
| indentured servant |
| plantation |
| settlers |
| slaves |
| territory |

B. Circle the best word or phrase to complete each sentence.

1. A (territory / plantation) was a large farm in the southern colonies.

2. (Settlers / Indentured servants) are people who come to a new place and decide to stay.

3. (Settlers / Slaves) from Africa had to work on the large farms.

4. People came from England to start a new (colony / plantation).

5. A large area of land is called a (plantation / territory).

6. (Settlers / Indentured servants) worked for several years to become free.

C. Draw an arrow between words that are related. Write four sentences to tell how they are related.

Jamestown	indentured servants	slaves	settlers
work hard	colony	freedom	plantations

1. _____

2. _____

3. _____

4. _____

Content Reading Strategy: Use What You Know

A. Complete the word web below with

- information about explorers (see Unit 4 for help).
- information you already know about Christopher Columbus.

Add more boxes if needed.

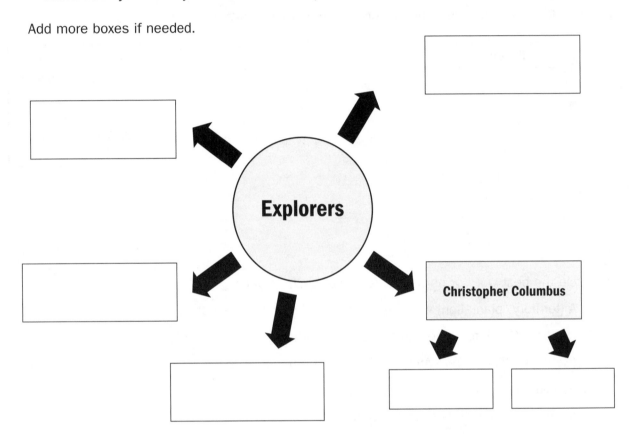

B. Compare your word web with a partner's. Add new information from your partner's web to your web. Use a different-colored pen.

C. Check the information on your web to make sure it is correct. Use your Student Book and other resources.

Unit 5: Lesson 1

Before You Read

SOCIAL STUDIES SKILLS

Using Visuals: Read a Chart

Read the chart. Then answer the questions.

Explorer	Country	Areas Explored	Dates of Exploration
John Cabot	England	North America: Newfoundland, Nova Scotia	1497–1498
Pedro Alvares Cabral	Portugal	Brazil	1500–1501
Christopher Columbus	Spain	Cuba, Dominican Republic, Haiti, coast of Central America	1492–1504
Hernán Cortés	Spain	Mexico, lower California	1518–1521
Francisco Pizarro	Spain	Pacific coast of South America, interior of Peru	1524–1533

1. Look at the dates of exploration. Which explorer sailed the earliest?

   _____

2. How many of these explorers explored for Spain? Who were they?

   _____

3. Who explored from 1497 to 1498? What country sent him?

   _____

4. Which explorer went to Mexico?

   _____

5. Which explorers did you already know about before reading this chart?

   _____

Using Visuals: Read a Chart

Complete the chart about Christopher Columbus's voyages. Use the information below.

1492–1493   Cuba, Hispañola

1493–1496   Dominica, Leeward Islands, Virgin Islands, Puerto Rico, Hispañola, Cuba

1498–1500   Trinidad, Margarita, Hispañola

1502–1504   Honduras, coast of Central America to Panama, Jamaica

Columbus's Voyages	Dates of Voyages	Areas Visited
First voyage		Cuba, Hispañola
	1493–1496	
Third voyage	1498–1500	
		Honduras, coast of Central America to Panama, Jamaica

Unit 5   Early United States

Unit 5: Lesson 1

More Review and Practice

VOCABULARY

Choose a word from the box to replace the words in *italics*. Write the word on the line.

| plantation | slaves | territory | colony | indentured servants |

1. Each group of settlers wanted to start a new *area that belongs to another country.*

   _____

2. A *southern farm* needed a lot of people to work in the fields. _____

3. Plantation owners brought *people who were forced to work* to the farms.

   _____

4. France and Britain both wanted a *large area of land.* _____

5. *People who worked to repay the cost of their voyage* worked four to seven years.

   _____

VOCABULARY IN CONTEXT

Complete each sentence. Use words from the box.

| plantations | slaves | territory | colony | settlers |

1. The first Puritan _____ went to Massachusetts.

2. Farmers grew tobacco and cotton on _____ in Virginia.

3. The Pilgrims and the Puritans each formed their own _____.

4. _____ worked very hard on the farms.

5. There was a lot of open _____ in North America.

TIMELINE CHECK

Use the timelines on pages 172–179 in your Student Book to answer the questions.

1. Did British rule in India begin before or after the French and Indian War started?

   _____

2. What happened in Lisbon, Portugal, in 1755?

   _____

Choose the best answer. Circle the letter.

1. Columbus was looking for _____.

   a. new fruits and vegetables   **b.** a faster route to Asia   **c.** a faster route to Greece

2. The English settlers found _____ living in North America.

   a. Native Americans   **b.** Native Asians   **c.** no one

3. One of the first English colonies was called _____.

   a. Williamsburg   **b.** New World   **c.** Jamestown

4. Pilgrims and Puritans are two groups of settlers who wanted _____.

   a. gold   **b.** plantations   **c.** religious freedom

5. In 1733 there were _____ English colonies in North America.

   a. thirteen   **b.** five   **c.** twelve

APPLY SOCIAL STUDIES SKILLS

Content Reading Strategy: Use What You Know

Use what you have learned about southern colonies and slavery to think about what happened next with slavery. Add your ideas to the box on the right.

What I Know
• Plantations needed workers.
• Plantation owners started buying Africans to work as slaves.
• Some people thought slavery was wrong.

What I Think Happened Next with Slavery

Using Visuals: Read a Chart

Look at the chart on page 181 in your Student Book. Then answer the questions.

1. Who made something for people to wear? _____

2. Who made something for people to eat with? _____

3. Who made something for people to use on wagons? _____

4. Who made something for people to read? _____

5. Who made tools for people to use? _____

Unit 5: Lesson 2

Before You Read

VOCABULARY

revolt	document	representatives	treaty	independence	tax

A. Write the key words next to the correct clues.

something written   **1.** _____   **2.** _____

something to do with the government   **3.** _____   **4.** _____

a strong protest   **5.** _____

something to do with freedom   **6.** _____

B. Write three sentences describing the pictures. Use key words in your sentences.

1. _____

2. _____

3. _____

C. Write T for *true* or F for *false*. Correct the sentences that are false.

_____ **1.** An official letter from your school is a kind of document.

_____ **2.** If a country wants independence, it wants to be a colony.

_____ **3.** A tax is land you give to the government.

_____ **4.** A treaty is a written agreement between countries.

_____ **5.** Representatives in the government are not elected.

Content Reading Strategy: Look for Cause and Effect

Look at the pairs of events listed below. Decide which event is a cause and which is an effect. Write them under the correct column.

- Puritans settled in Massachusetts.
- Puritans did not have religious freedom in England.

- Settlers in Jamestown did not have enough food during the first winter.
- Many settlers died.

- Europe became interested in the New World.
- Columbus returned from his first voyage to tell about new lands and peoples.

Cause	Effect

Unit 5: Lesson 2

Before You Read

SOCIAL STUDIES SKILLS

Content Reading Strategy: Look for Cause and Effect

Complete the missing information from the boxes. Write a cause (why something happened) or an effect (what happened).

Cause	Effect
1.	Columbus made several voyages to the New World.
2. Colonists were not prepared for their first winter.	
3.	People were brought from Africa to be slaves.
4. Both France and Britain wanted more territory.	
5.	Life changed for Native Americans.

Using Visuals: Read a Chart

Read the chart. Then answer the questions.

Estimated Colonial Population	
Year	Total Population: White and African (rounded to the nearest 100)
1630	4,600
1650	50,400
1670	111,900
1690	210,400
1710	331,700
1730	629,400
1750	1,170,800
1770	2,148,100

1. What is this chart about?

_____

2. The years on the chart increase by how many for each row?

_____

3. How many years does this chart cover?

_____

4. What was the total increase in population from 1630 to 1770?

_____

5. The colonial population almost doubled every twenty years. Why do you think this happened?

_____

Unit 5: Lesson 2

More Review and Practice

VOCABULARY

Complete each sentence. Use words from the box. There is one extra word.

| document | revolt | independence | treaty | tax | representatives |

1. In protest against new taxes, the colonists began a _____.

2. The U.S. Constitution is an important _____ in American history.

3. The thirteen colonies wanted _____ from England.

4. At the end of the War for Independence, England and the united colonies signed a

   _____.

5. In 1787 _____ met in Philadelphia to write the Constitution.

VOCABULARY IN CONTEXT

Circle the best word to complete each sentence.

1. The colonists paid a (revolt / tax) on things they bought.

2. A birth certificate is an important (treaty / document).

3. We elect (representatives / independence) to our government.

4. The angry colonists decided to (revolt / tax) against England.

5. The U.S. Constitution was written after the War for (Representatives / Independence).

TIMELINE CHECK

Use the timelines on pages 186–193 in your Student Book to answer the questions.

1. What events happened in 1750?

   _____

2. Where were the Russians exploring? In what year was that?

   _____

3. Was Los Angeles founded before or after the Boston Tea Party?

   _____

4. When was the first successful hot air balloon?

   _____

Match the parts of the sentence. Write the letter.

_____ 1. The Boston Tea Party

_____ 2. The Declaration of Independence

_____ 3. Many colonists wanted

_____ 4. Representatives from most of
the colonies

_____ 5. George Washington

a. to be independent from England.

b. was a protest against British taxes.

c. became the first U.S. president.

d. was the document signed on July 4, 1776.

e. met in Philadelphia to decide about a revolt.

APPLY SOCIAL STUDIES SKILLS

Content Reading Strategy: Look for Cause and Effect

Look at the illustration. Then answer the questions. Write complete sentences.

1. Who are the people in this picture?

   _____

   _____

2. What was the cause of their actions?

   _____

   _____

3. What effect did their actions have on the British?

   _____

   _____

Using Visuals: Read a Chart

Look at the chart on page 195 in your Student Book. Then answer the questions.

1. What two groups are represented in this chart?

   _____

2. Does this chart show cause and effect?

   _____

Unit 5

Unit Review

VOCABULARY

Draw an arrow between words that are related. Write five sentences to tell how they are related.

treaty	president	tax	independence	tobacco
government	document	colony	plantations	protest

1. _____

2. _____

3. _____

4. _____

5. _____

VOCABULARY IN CONTEXT

Complete the chart. Use a dictionary to help you.

Singular Noun	Plural Noun	Verb
government	governments	to govern
1.	settlers	
2.		to tax
3. representative		
4. colony		
5.	revolts	

Choose one word from each row above. Write a sentence using that word.

1. _____

2. _____

3. _____

4. _____

5. _____

Put the events in the correct order. Number them from 1 to 5.

_____ The French surrendered to the British to end the French and Indian War.

_____ Jamestown started its own government.

_____ The colonists and the British signed the Treaty of Paris.

_____ Colonists threw tea into the water to protest higher taxes.

_____ Representatives signed the U.S. Constitution.

APPLY SOCIAL STUDIES SKILLS

Using Visuals: Read a Chart

Read the chart. Then answer the questions.

Jobs in the Colonies	What They Did
Wigmaker	Made wigs for men
Miller	Made grain into flour
Printer	Printed books and newspapers
Apothecary	Provided medical treatment Gave medicine Delivered babies
Wheelwright	Made wheels
Blacksmith	Made things out of iron

1. Which colonial jobs did you learn about in your Student Book?

_____

_____

_____

2. Which colonial jobs are new to you?

_____

_____

_____

3. Which job do you think was the most important? Why?

_____

_____

_____

_____

EXTENSION PROJECT

Imagine you are a colonist. Make a poster to protest about something in the colonies (taxes, slavery, British soldiers, etc.). Explain your poster to the class.

Unit 5

Writing Skills

WRITE A THREE-PARAGRAPH ESSAY

Use the outline below to write a three-paragraph essay. The first paragraph is already written for you on page 96. Add your own second and third paragraphs to complete the essay. Remember to include details and to write a concluding sentence.

Causes of the War for Independence

   I. The Proclamation of 1763

      A. King of England said the colonists could not move west

      B. Many colonists did not obey

   II. The British were taxing the colonists more and more

      A. Stamp Act of 1765

      B. Taxes on tea, sugar, and molasses

      C. Colonists had no representation in the British government

   III. The Intolerable Acts of 1774

      A. Took away many rights of the colonists

      B. Closed Boston Harbor

      C. Colonists became very unhappy with British rule and wanted independence

There were several causes of the War for Independence fought by the colonists against the British. In 1763 the king of England made a new rule. He said that the colonists could not live west of the Appalachian Mountains. He called this new rule the Proclamation of 1763. The colonists were not happy about what the king said. They decided not to obey this rule.

Unit 6: Lesson 1

Before You Read

VOCABULARY

A. Match the key words with a definition. Write the letter.

_____ **1.** pioneers   **a.** a person who moves to a new country

_____ **2.** gold rush   **b.** a group of wagons

_____ **3.** tribe   **c.** the first people in a new place

_____ **4.** immigrant   **d.** a community of people with a common culture

_____ **5.** wagon train   **e.** the business of making things to sell

_____ **6.** industry   **f.** a period when people moved to California

B. Write four sentences using a key word and its definition.

1. _____

2. _____

3. _____

4. _____

C. Write T for *true* or F for *false.* Correct the sentences that are false.

_____ **1.** The gold rush was a new place.

_____ **2.** A tribe is a group of people with a common culture.

_____ **3.** A wagon train is a long line of cars.

_____ **4.** An immigrant moves to a new country.

_____ **5.** Many pioneers moved west toward California.

D. Circle the word that doesn't belong.

1. Native Americans	immigrants	railroads	China
2. gold rush	pioneers	tribe	California
3. tribe	community	Native American	factory
4. factories	gold rush	business	industry
5. pioneers	industry	wagon train	Great Plains

Content Reading Strategy: Compare and Contrast

A. Read the paragraph. Compare and contrast George Washington and Thomas Jefferson. Write your information in the Venn diagram below.

During the War for Independence, George Washington was the commander of the Continental Army. Washington was also a landowner and a farmer. He had slaves like most other landowners. After the war, he went back to his farm. Later, he helped to set up a new government. He helped to write the United States Constitution. George Washington became the first president of the United States.

Thomas Jefferson also helped to set up a new government. Like Washington, Jefferson helped to write the Constitution. Before the war, he wrote the Declaration of Independence, an important document that told England what the colonists wanted. Jefferson owned land, and slaves, and he was a farmer, too. Later, he became the third president of the United States. Both men were great leaders.

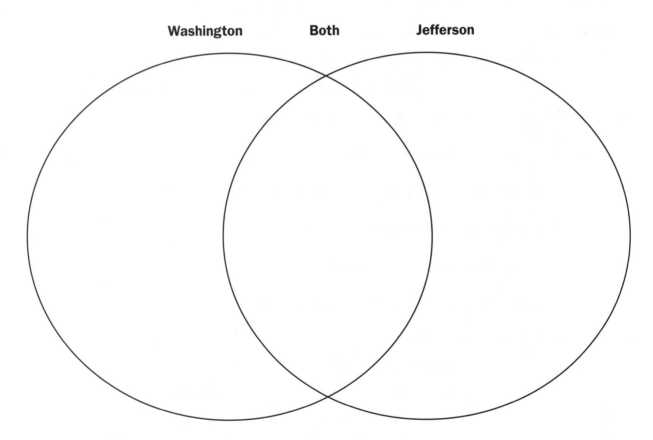

Washington   **Both**   **Jefferson**

B. Compare your Venn diagram with a partner's. Add any new information from your partner's diagram to your diagram. Use a different-colored pen.

Unit 6: Lesson 1

Before You Read

SOCIAL STUDIES SKILLS

Content Reading Strategy: Compare and Contrast

A. Read the paragraph. Compare and contrast a Native American tribe and a colony of settlers. Write your information in the Venn diagram below.

There were differences and similarities between a Native American tribe and a colony of settlers. They both had a system of government to make laws. They both had leaders to help run their governments. Each group was a community and had members who participated in the community. The members were men, women, and children. Native American tribes were already living in the New World when the settlers came. The settlers were immigrants. The tribes knew how to survive in the New World. The settlers did not know how to survive. They were just learning. The people of the tribes showed the people of the colony how to work the land.

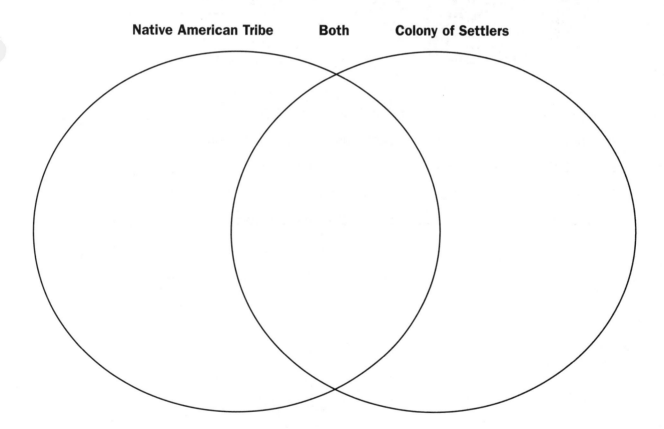

Native American Tribe   **Both**   **Colony of Settlers**

B. Compare your Venn diagram with a partner's. Add any new information from your partner's diagram to your diagram. Use a different-colored pen.

Using Visuals: Read a Graph

Read the circle graph below. Then answer the questions.

The Largest Groups to Immigrate to the United States between 1851 and 1860

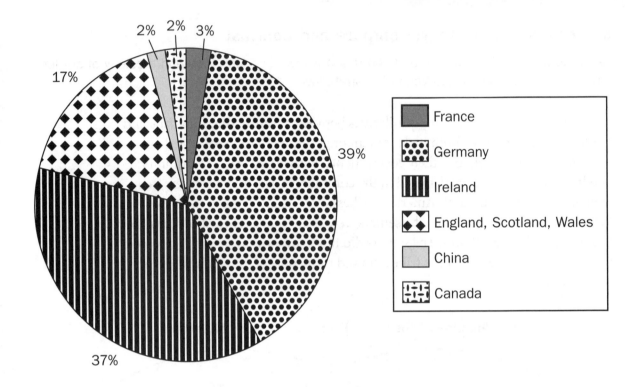

1. What country was the largest group of immigrants from? _____

2. What country was the second-largest group of immigrants from? _____

3. What percentage of immigrants came from China? _____

4. What immigrant group was from North America? _____

5. Why do you think these groups came to the United States?

_____

_____

Unit 6: Lesson 1

More Review and Practice

VOCABULARY

Complete the puzzle. Use key words. Write the secret word.

1. The _____ traveled on the Oregon Trail.
   __ __ __ __ __ __ __ __

2. They traveled to California in a _____.
   Ⓞ__ __ __ __   __ __ __ __ __

3. A Shoshone _____ helped Lewis and Clark.
   __ __ __ Ⓞ

4. _____ helped to build the railroads.
   __ __ __ __ __ __ __ __ __ __

5. In 1848, "gold fever" started the _____.
   __ __ __ __   __ __ Ⓞ __

6. Many people in the North worked in _____.
   __ __ __ __ __ Ⓞ __ __

Secret word: __ __ __ __

VOCABULARY IN CONTEXT

Complete each sentence. Use words from the box. There is one extra word.

| tribes | pioneers | immigrants | wagon trains | gold rush |

From the 1840s to the 1870s, more than half a million **(1)** _____
traveled west on the Oregon Trail. Most travelers went in **(2)** _____
because it was safer. Some Native American **(3)** _____ helped the
pioneers, but some attacked them. After Chinese and Irish **(4)** _____
finished building the transcontinental railroad, the Oregon Trail was not used much.

TIMELINE CHECK

Use the timelines on pages 206–213 in your Student Book. Write T for *true* or F for *false*.

_____ **1.** The United States bought the Oregon Trail from France in 1803.

_____ **2.** The Mexican army defeated the American settlers at the Alamo in 1836.

_____ **3.** The gold rush began in California in 1848.

_____ **4.** Napoleon III became emperor of France in 1851.

_____ **5.** In 1847 Samuel F. Morse sent the first telegram.

Choose the best answer. Circle the letter.

1. Many northerners wanted to _____ slavery.

   a. buy   **b.** abolish   **c.** increase

2. The _____ caused pioneers to migrate west.

   a. discovery of gold   **b.** Pony Express   **c.** buffalo

3. Lewis and Clark were looking for _____.

   a. gold   **b.** a water route   **c.** slaves

4. Frederick Douglass was an African-American _____.

   a. pioneer   **b.** tribe   **c.** abolitionist

5. The _____ was a mail system used by western pioneers.

   a. Mississippi River   **b.** gold rush   **c.** Pony Express

APPLY SOCIAL STUDIES SKILLS

Content Reading Strategy: Compare and Contrast

Read the paragraph below. Use the information to make a Venn diagram in your notebook. Be sure to put headings on your diagram.

There were differences and similarities between the Great Plains Indians and the settlers. The Indians lived in tents called teepees, while the settlers lived in houses made of stone and wood. The Plains Indians moved around. The settlers stayed in one place to farm the land. They both needed food, water, and shelter to survive. They both made laws to govern their people. They both used the land.

Using Visuals: Read a Graph

Look at the circle graph on page 215 in your Student Book. Then answer these questions.

1. Where did most slaves go? _____

2. Where did the fewest slaves go? _____

3. Who bought more slaves, Portugal or Spain? _____

4. What percentage of slaves went to Spanish America? _____

5. What do the numbers in the graph represent? _____

Unit 6: Lesson 2

Before You Read

VOCABULARY

A. What am I? Write words from the box next to the correct clues.

| battle | fort | railroads | Confederacy | Union | Mason-Dixon Line |

1. I defend people from danger.   _____

2. I am an imaginary line between the North and the South.   _____

3. I am a fight between two armies.   _____

4. I am the North during the Civil War.   _____

5. I am the South during the Civil War.   _____

6. I am a means of transportation across a country.   _____

B. Write three sentences describing the picture. Use key words in your sentences.

1. _____

2. _____

3. _____

Content Reading Strategy: Draw Conclusions

Read the paragraph carefully. Look at the graphic organizer and study the clues. Then write your conclusion.

During the twenty-five years of westward expansion, more than half a million pioneers traveled west. It was a long, difficult journey on the Oregon Trail. Many people never arrived on the west coast. In 1869 builders completed the transcontinental railroad. It connected the east coast and the west coast of the United States.

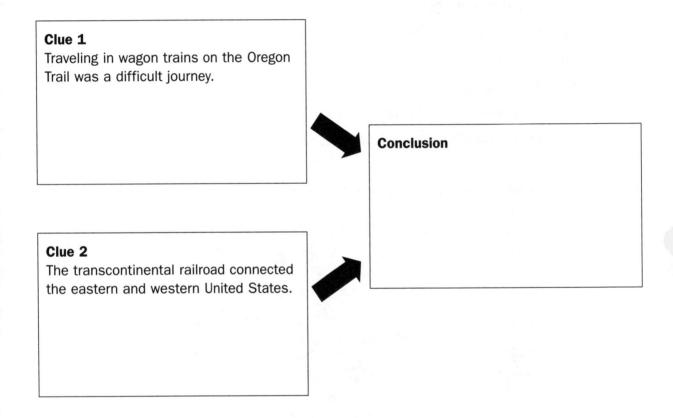

Clue 1
Traveling in wagon trains on the Oregon Trail was a difficult journey.

Clue 2
The transcontinental railroad connected the eastern and western United States.

Conclusion

Unit 6: Lesson 2

Before You Read

Content Reading Strategy: Draw Conclusions

Read the paragraph carefully. Look at the graphic organizer and study the clues. Write your conclusion.

The national government of the United States started making currency, or coins, after the War for Independence. For a long time, though, people still used foreign coins. The U.S. government did not have much gold or silver to use to make coins, so people used Spanish coins. Then gold was discovered in California in 1848.

Clue 1
The U.S. government needed to have its own currency.

Clue 2
People in the United States used foreign coins instead of U.S. money.

Conclusion

Clue 3
Then gold was discovered in California.

Using Visuals: Read a Graph

Look at the bar graph. Then answer the questions below.

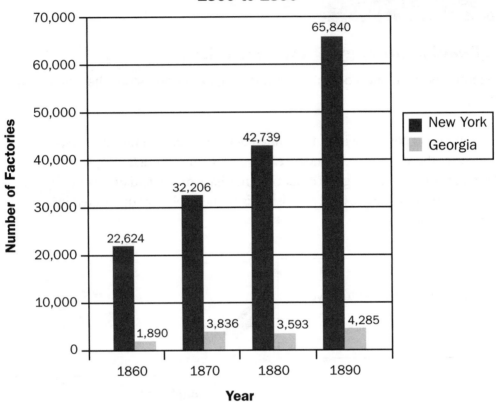

Factory Growth in New York and Georgia, 1860 to 1890

1. Which state had more factories in 1860?

   _____

2. Which state had fewer factories in 1890?

   _____

3. Did Georgia increase the amount of factories from 1860 to 1890? By how much?

   _____

4. Did New York increase the amount of factories from 1860 to 1890? By how much?

   _____

5. Why do you think there were more factories in New York than in Georgia?

   _____

Unit 6: Lesson 2

More Review and Practice

VOCABULARY

Circle the best word to complete each sentence.

1. The northern and southern armies fought many (states / battles).

2. The (fort / Mason-Dixon Line) separated the North and the South.

3. A (fort / battle) protected the soldiers.

4. The southern states formed the (Union / Confederacy).

5. The northern states formed the (Union / Confederacy).

VOCABULARY IN CONTEXT

Write T for *true* or F for *false.* Correct the sentences that are false.

_____ 1. The Confederacy won the Civil War.

_____ 2. Railroads provided better transportation than covered wagons.

_____ 3. The Civil War began with a battle at Fort Sumter.

_____ 4. The southern states wanted to be called the Union.

_____ 5. The Mason-Dixon Line was a new railroad.

TIMELINE CHECK

Use the timelines on pages 220–227 in your Student Book to answer the questions.

1. What event happened in Asia in 1876?

_____

2. What war began in 1898?

_____

3. When did the Franco-Prussian War begin?

_____

4. When were the first typewriters made?

_____

5. What happened in 1890?

_____

Choose the best answer. Circle the letter.

1. _____ was abolished in the United States after the Civil War.

   a. Voting   **b.** Slavery   **c.** The Confederacy

2. _____ was president of the United States during the Civil War.

   a. George Washington   **b.** Thomas Jefferson   **c.** Abraham Lincoln

3. The period after the Civil War was called _____.

   a. Independence   **b.** Reconstruction   **c.** Secession

4. In the late 1860s, the U.S. government wanted to put Native Americans _____.

   a. on reservations   **b.** on farms   **c.** in cities

5. The _____ helped the U.S. economy grow and created new jobs.

   a. Civil War   **b.** wagon trains   **c.** railroads

APPLY SOCIAL STUDIES SKILLS

Content Reading Strategy: Draw Conclusions

Read the paragraph. Then read the clues and write a conclusion.

During the Industrial Revolution, many Americans went to work in factories. They left their small towns and farms to work in the cities. They worked and lived in terrible conditions. Many men, women, and children had to work twelve to fourteen hours a day in low-paying jobs.

Clue 1
Many Americans went to work in factories.

Clue 2
They left their small towns and farms to work and live in cities.

Conclusion

Using Visuals: Read a Graph

Look at the graph on page 229 in your Student Book. Write T for *true* or F for *false.*

_____ 1. There were 5,000 more miles of track in 1845 than in 1840.

_____ 2. In 1850 and 1860, there were the same miles of railroad tracks.

_____ 3. The miles of tracks probably continued to increase after 1860.

Unit 6

Unit Review

VOCABULARY

Match a word or phrase in Column A with a phrase in Column B. Write the letter.
Then write sentences below.

Column A	Column B
_____ 1. Confederacy	**a.** a person who moves to a new country
_____ 2. immigrant	**b.** a fight between two armies
_____ 3. railroads	**c.** the business of making and selling goods
_____ 4. pioneers	**d.** a long line of wagons
_____ 5. industry	**e.** the first people to settle a new place
_____ 6. Union	**f.** a fast means of transportation
_____ 7. gold rush	**g.** a structure that protects people from attacks
_____ 8. wagon train	**h.** southern states
_____ 9. battle	**i.** northern states
_____ 10. fort	**j.** caused people to move west

1. _____

2. _____

3. _____

4. _____

5. _____

VOCABULARY IN CONTEXT

Complete the paragraph. Use words from the box. There is one extra word.

pioneers	industry	battle	immigrants	railroads	tribes

(1) _____ were important to the growth of **(2)** _____
in the United States. Railroad construction changed the way people lived, including
Native American **(3)** _____ . **(4)** _____ from China and
Ireland built a lot of the railroad tracks. Then they stayed in the United States to live and
work. They also became **(5)** _____ and settled new areas in the West.

Put the events in the correct order. Number them from 1 to 6.

_____ General Lee surrendered.

_____ The Reconstruction period ended.

_____ George Washington retired as president of the United States.

_____ Gold was discovered in California.

_____ Chief Joseph's father signed a treaty with the U.S. government.

_____ The battle at Fort Sumter began the Civil War.

APPLY SOCIAL STUDIES SKILLS

Content Reading Strategy: Compare and Contrast

Read the paragraph. Use the information to make a Venn diagram in your notebook. Be sure to put headings on your diagram.

There were differences and similarities between the North and the South. The North and the South were both under the same federal government. There were cities and ports in both areas. Both economies depended on trade. The North and the South used new inventions to expand their economies. However, they had differences. The North was heavily industrial, with many factories. The South was agricultural, with many plantations. The South supported slavery. The North opposed slavery.

EXTENSION PROJECT

Imagine you are a pioneer moving west with your family. In order to get there, you have to travel the Oregon Trail with many others.

- Make a list of the things you will need to take on your trip.

- Write a journal of what happens to you during the trip: attacks, diseases, bad weather, meeting friendly tribes. Use the Internet, books, or CD-ROMs to find information about life on the Oregon Trail.

Unit 6

Writing Skills

REVISE A THREE-PARAGRAPH ESSAY

A. Read the essay below. There are some things wrong with it. Then answer the questions about the essay.

Slave Families

The slave trade brought Africans to the United States as slaves. The southern states depended heavily on slaves to do the work on the plantations. This divided the nation because most northerners did not approve of slavery. The migration of Europeans to the Americas began in the 1500s. Entire tribes and families were sold and taken across the Atlantic to the Americas and the Caribbean islands.

Many Africans died during the long voyage. But this was not the end of the trip. Some slaves were sent to non-Spanish Caribbean islands, some were sent to Brazil, some were sent to Spanish America, and some were sent to British America. Lewis and Clark traveled west across the United States to find a water route to the Pacific Ocean. The first slaves were brought to Jamestown in 1619.

Many northerners did not like the South because of slavery. Southerners wanted the North to leave them alone. The North wanted to abolish slavery in the United States. The South wanted to keep it. They did not agree, and this was one reason for the American Civil War.

1. Does the essay have a main idea? _____

2. Does the essay need a better title? _____

3. Are the ideas in the best order and related to the topic? _____

4. What sentences would you take out of the first and second paragraphs?

_____

_____

_____

_____

_____

5. Does this essay have a beginning, middle, and end? _____

B. Now revise the essay and make it better. Write your revision in your notebook.

C. Exchange revised essays with a partner. Answer the questions below about your partner's essay.

Questions about the Essay

1. Does the essay have a main idea? _____

2. Does the essay have an appropriate title? _____

3. Are the ideas in the best order and related to the topic? _____

4. Are there specific details and examples? _____

5. Does this essay have a beginning, middle, and end? _____

Unit 7: Lesson 1

Before You Read

VOCABULARY

A. Match the key words with a definition. Write the letter.

_____ **1.** assassination	**a.** not having a job
_____ **2.** atomic bomb	**b.** underwater boats
_____ **3.** dictator	**c.** a political murder
_____ **4.** Holocaust	**d.** a leader with absolute power
_____ **5.** submarines	**e.** a deadly weapon
_____ **6.** unemployment	**f.** the large killing during World War II

B. Write four sentences using a key word and its definition.

1. _____

2. _____

3. _____

4. _____

C. Circle the best word to complete each sentence.

1. Archduke Franz Ferdinand's (atomic bomb / assassination) started World War I.

2. The (Holocaust / unemployment) occurred during World War II.

3. (Dictators / Submarines) were a new invention in World War I.

4. (Employment / Unemployment) means people are without jobs.

5. A (worker / dictator) has absolute power over all the people.

D. Circle the word that doesn't belong.

1. assassination	murder	jobs	political
2. submarines	large killing	Holocaust	concentration camp
3. dictator	airplanes	boats	submarines
4. atomic bomb	weapon	unemployment	deadly
5. Hitler	dictator	absolute power	submarines

Content Reading Strategy: Summarize

Read the paragraph below about the invention of submarines. Then summarize it in your own words. Remember that a summary includes the main idea and the most important details.

Submarines in World War I

The first time that submarines were used in a war was in World War I. The Germans built submarines, called U-boats. They were named U-boats because the German navy had a system of naming each submarine with the letter *U* and a number. The *U* was for *Unterseeboot* (undersea boat), the German word for *submarine*. The U-boats operated on the water's surface using regular engines. Underwater they changed to battery power. That meant they could approach a ship quietly. The German U-boats were a destructive force in the war. The American submarines entered World War I after the Germans attacked U.S. ships.

Summary

_____

_____

_____

_____

_____

_____

_____

_____

Unit 7: Lesson 1

Before You Read

SOCIAL STUDIES SKILLS

Content Reading Strategy: Summarize

Read the paragraph below about the Holocaust. Then summarize it in your own words. Remember that a summary includes the main idea and the most important details.

The Holocaust

The Holocaust refers to Nazi Germany's mass-murder of various ethnic, religious, and national groups during World War II. This mass-murder started in 1941 and continued through 1945. The Jewish people of Europe were the main targets of the Holocaust, but other groups suffered as well. These other groups included Slavs, Poles, Romanys, disabled people, Jehovah's Witnesses, Soviet prisoners of war, and political activists. The Nazis put these groups of people in concentration camps, where they were used for slave labor or killed. Historians estimate that 12 million people were killed. The full story of the Holocaust was not known until after the war.

Summary

_____

_____

_____

_____

_____

_____

_____

Building Research Skills: Use Print Resources

Look at the reference tools below. Then answer the questions.

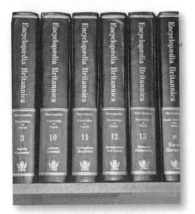

▲ Encyclopedias

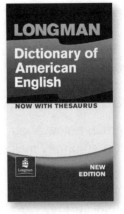

▲ Dictionary

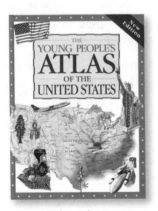

▲ Atlas

▲ Periodicals

1. What are print resources used for?

   _____

2. Where would you look for the political borders of Asian countries?

   _____

3. If you want to find out about the life of Adolf Hitler or Archduke Franz Ferdinand, what print resource would you use?

   _____

4. Where would you look for information about what is happening in your home country today?

   _____

5. If you want to find out whether a word is an adjective, a noun, or a verb, where would you look?

   _____

Unit 7: Lesson 1

More Review and Practice

VOCABULARY

Complete the puzzle. Use key words. Write the secret word.

1. a leader with absolute power   — — — — ◯ — — —

2. the mass killing of people in
   Nazi Germany   — — ◯ — — — — — —

3. the absence of jobs   — — — — — ◯ — — — — —

4. It destroyed Hiroshima.   — — — — ◯ — — — —

5. boats that go underwater   — — — — — — — — ◯ — —

6. a political murder   — — — — — ◯ — — — — — — —

Secret word: ___ ___ ___ ___ ___ ___

VOCABULARY IN CONTEXT

Complete the paragraph. Use words from the box. There is one extra word.

| dictator | Holocaust | submarine | unemployment | atomic bomb | assassination |

   The (1) _____ of Archduke Franz Ferdinand was a political killing. It

started World War I. The Central Powers lost the war. After the war, Hitler came to power.

He became a (2) _____. He had absolute power. He started another war.

He used an invention called a (3) _____ in this war. He also wanted to

build a deadly weapon called the (4) _____. During World War II, the Nazis

organized mass killings called the (5) _____.

TIMELINE CHECK

Use the timelines on pages 240–247 in your Student Book to answer the questions.

1. What happened in 1918?

   _____

2. What happened in 1929?

   _____

Choose the best answer. Circle the letter.

1. Germany, the Austro-Hungarian Empire, and Turkey were called the _____.

    a. Allies   **b.** Central Powers   **c.** League of Nations

2. In 1917 the United States entered _____.

    a. the Spanish-American War   **b.** World War II   **c.** World War I

3. Adolf Hitler was the head of the _____ Party in Germany.

    a. Democratic   **b.** Independent   **c.** Nazi

4. The period of time after the U.S. stock market collapsed is called _____.

    a. the Great Depression   **b.** the Progressive Era   **c.** World War I

5. In 1945 fifty countries signed the _____ Charter.

    a. New York   **b.** Bill of Rights   **c.** United Nations

Content Reading Strategy: Summarize

Reread page 244 in your Student Book about the Great Depression. Write a summary below.

_____

_____

_____

_____

_____

_____

_____

Building Research Skills: Use Print Resources

Answer the questions. Use words from the box.

a dictionary   an encyclopedia   a periodical   an atlas

1. Where would you find the meaning of *suffrage*? _____

2. Where could you find more information about Franklin D. Roosevelt? _____

3. Where would you find information about buying computers? _____

4. Where would you find out what states border California? _____

Unit 7: Lesson 2

Before You Read

VOCABULARY

A. Circle the best word to complete each sentence.

1. (Communism / Liberty) is a political system in which the government owns everything.

2. Oil and gold are natural (economy / resources).

3. (Economy / Democracy) refers to money, business, and products in a country.

4. When people are able to elect their leaders, it is called a (democracy / party).

5. (Global / Terrorism) is a violent political action committed by people.

6. Nuclear weapons are a (global / resource) threat.

B. Draw an arrow between words or phrases that are related. Write four sentences to tell how they are related.

terrorism	free elections
resources	hijacking
economy	oil and gold
democracy	money and business

1. _____

2. _____

3. _____

4. _____

C. Write T for *true* or F for *false*. Correct the sentences that are false.

_____ **1.** Diamonds and oil are not resources from the earth.

_____ **2.** Communism is a system in which you can have free elections.

_____ **3.** In a democracy people elect their leaders.

_____ **4.** A global economy means that most countries are trading with each other.

_____ **5.** Terrorism is not a political action.

Content Reading Strategy: Understand Fact and Opinion

Read the paragraph below. Then answer the questions.

The Era of Franklin Delano Roosevelt

Franklin Delano Roosevelt was the only U.S. president elected to four terms of office. He became president in 1933 during the Great Depression. Roosevelt started several economic and social assistance programs, called the New Deal, to help get the country out of the Depression. Under Roosevelt, the Social Security Act was passed. Some people believe the New Deal programs were successful, while other people believe they did not go far enough in improving the economic situation. During Roosevelt's third term of office, the United States entered World War II. Perhaps Roosevelt did not want to go to war, but after the attack on Pearl Harbor he had no choice. Roosevelt sent Japanese Americans to internment camps. That might have been a mistake. People were very divided in their opinions about the internment camps.

1. What are two facts in the paragraph?

   Fact: _____

   _____

   Fact: _____

   _____

2. What are two opinions in the paragraph?

   Opinion: _____

   _____

   Opinion: _____

   _____

3. Where can you check the facts in the paragraph?

   _____

4. What words or phrases helped you identify the opinions?

   _____

5. What is *your* opinion about Franklin D. Roosevelt?

   _____

   _____

Unit 7: Lesson 2

Before You Read

Content Reading Strategy: Understand Fact and Opinion

Read the paragraphs below. Then answer the questions.

Popular Communication Tools

Home computers and cellular phones are two consumer products that have changed the way most people communicate. Perhaps people never imagined they would be so popular, but they are.

The Internet started in 1969 as a U.S. government project to help researchers communicate with each other. This network became more public after Tim Berners-Lee created the World Wide Web. Many people believe the Internet is the best invention ever. Others think children spend too much time on it.

Cellular phones used to be large and expensive. They are now low-cost and small. This change has happened in less than twenty years. According to the Scarborough study, for the year 2002, almost 62 percent of American adults owned a cellular phone. Cellular phones are used around the world, so there might be millions and millions of users. Perhaps in the future every person will carry one.

1. What are two facts in the paragraphs?

   Fact: _____

   _____

   Fact: _____

   _____

2. What are two opinions in the paragraphs?

   Opinion: _____

   _____

   Opinion: _____

   _____

3. Where can you check the facts in the paragraph? _____

4. What words or phrases helped you identify the opinions?

   _____

5. What is *your* opinion about home computers and cellular phones?

   _____

Building Research Skills: Use Technology Resources

Look at the pictures below. Then answer the questions.

▲ CD-ROMs

▲ A computerized catalog

1. What kind of information can you find on a CD-ROM?

   _____

2. What kind of information can you find in a computerized catalog?

   _____

3. Which technology resource would you use to find a book about the Internet?

   _____

4. Which technology resource would you use to find information on Nelson Mandela?

   _____

5. Which technology resources have you used at school?

   _____

Unit 7: Lesson 2

More Review and Practice

VOCABULARY

Match the parts of the sentence. Write the letter.

_____ **1.** Communism   **a.** refers to money, business, and products in a country.

_____ **2.** Economy   **b.** are sources of wealth such as gold or oil.

_____ **3.** Resources   **c.** means worldwide.

_____ **4.** Global   **d.** is a political system in which the government owns and controls everything.

_____ **5.** Democracy   **e.** is a violent political action by a person or group.

_____ **6.** Terrorism   **f.** is a political system in which people vote to elect their leaders.

VOCABULARY IN CONTEXT

Write T for *true* or F for *false*. Correct the sentences that are false.

_____ **1.** Terrorism is a threat to all nations.

_____ **2.** In a democracy, people are free to choose their leaders.

_____ **3.** Natural resources are not important to a country.

_____ **4.** Today we have a global economy.

_____ **5.** Communism is a natural resource.

TIMELINE CHECK

Use the timelines on pages 254–261 in your Student Book to answer the questions.

1. What happened in 1948?

_____

2. Who was assassinated in 1963?

_____

3. What unit event occurred in 1969?

_____

4. What disaster occurred in 1986?

_____

CHECK YOUR UNDERSTANDING

Choose the best answer. Circle the letter.

1. An invisible line called the _____ divided the Soviet Union from the West.

    a. Iron Curtain   **b.** Berlin Wall   **c.** Mason-Dixon Line

2. The Cold War began after _____.

    a. World War I   **b.** the Civil War   **c.** World War II

3. In the 1960s the United States became involved in _____.

    a. World War II   **b.** the Vietnam War   **c.** the Korean War

4. Countries in Central and South America have experienced _____.

    a. many political changes   **b.** no changes   **c.** minor changes

5. Africa has _____ such as oil and diamonds.

    a. manufacturing   **b.** civil wars   **c.** natural resources

APPLY SOCIAL STUDIES SKILLS

Content Reading Strategy: Understand Fact and Opinion

Read the sentences. Write O for *opinion* or F for *fact*.

_____ **1.** The United States and Great Britain have democratic governments.

_____ **2.** Some people believe communism is the best form of government.

_____ **3.** The Soviets built the Berlin Wall in 1961.

_____ **4.** Many people thought the Vietnam War was wrong.

_____ **5.** The Allies defeated Germany in World War II.

Building Research Skills: Use Technology Resources

Which technology resource would you use to find the items below?

the Internet   CD-ROMs   a computerized catalog

1. video clips of twentieth-century historical events   _____

2. the author, title, and subject of a book   _____

3. a speech by President John F. Kennedy   _____

4. airline tickets   _____

5. educational games   _____

Unit 7

Unit Review

VOCABULARY

Draw arrows between pairs of words that are related. Write sentences to tell how they are related.

resources	terrorism
World War I	communism
global	oil and diamonds
Cuba	World War II
unemployment	submarines
atomic bomb	the Great Depression

1. _____

2. _____

3. _____

4. _____

5. _____

6. _____

VOCABULARY IN CONTEXT

Complete the paragraph. Use words from the box. There is one extra word.

dictators	democracy	assassinations	global	resources

The twentieth century was a time of important changes within and between countries.

(1) _____ of leaders in the United States such as John F. Kennedy and

Martin Luther King Jr. shocked the world. (2) _____ in Central and South

America were overthrown in civil wars. Then the world began moving toward cooperation

between countries to form a (3) _____ economy. People are realizing that

we need to share our (4) _____.

Put the events in the correct order. Number them from 1 to 6. Find the dates for these events. Make a timeline below.

_____ The Cultural Revolution took place in China.

_____ The Wright brothers made their first successful flight.

_____ Apartheid ended in South Africa.

_____ The stock market collapsed.

_____ Color television was invented.

_____ The United States entered World War II.

APPLY SOCIAL STUDIES SKILLS

Content Reading Strategy: Understand Fact and Opinion

Reread pages 240–241 in your Student Book. Then read the sentences below. Write O for _opinion_ or F for _fact_.

_____ 1. In the early 1900s, women in many Western countries won the right to vote.

_____ 2. Perhaps women should not have received the right to vote.

_____ 3. During the Progressive Era, there were many new inventions.

_____ 4. I think people felt hopeful at the beginning of the 1900s.

_____ 5. Industrial production was increasing.

EXTENSION PROJECT

Use print and technology resources to find information on one of the following topics:

- apartheid
- the breakup of the Soviet Union
- the assassination of President Kennedy
- the Cuban Revolution
- the first man on the moon
- Mother Teresa

Make an outline of your information. List the resources you used to find your information.

Unit 7

Writing Skills

EDIT AND PUBLISH A THREE-PARAGRAPH ESSAY

A. Read the essay below. Use the proofreading marks on page 267 in your Student Book to edit this essay.

After Germany lost wwi they signed the Treaty of versailles. This treaty ended Worl War I. The Germans had to promise to make payments to all the nations that were involved in the fighting. France demanded that Germany never again armies build. They also lost many territories. The people German felt very upset

These sanctions were taking a huje piece of the German economy. People were angry. This general anger continued to growe. They resented the allied powers for not forgiving them and giving them a chance to rejoin   Europe. The economy went from bad to worse. unEmployment got higher. Feeelings of humiliation continued to grow until German people began to blame Jewish citizens and other people for they're problems.

One man took advantage of all this. Adolf Hitler, a painter from Germany, decided to form the nazi Party. He told the people that he was the men to give them revenge against their European enemies. He told them that if he were elected chancellor, he would make their lives better. Instead, when he was elected leader he became a dictator. He declared war on Europe. The German Army invaded Poland, then Norway and denmark, and later France. this was the beginning of Worle War II.

B. Compare your edits with a classmate's. Make additional changes, if necessary.

C. Write an essay. Use the outline from your Extension Project on page 126 of this Workbook, or choose a new topic. After completing your essay, revise and edit it. Exchange essays with another student. Make suggestions and proofreading edits to your classmate's essay. Then revise your essay again if needed. Read the final essay aloud with a small group or in front of the class.

Understanding the Past Tense

Simple Past Tense of Regular Verbs

A. Write the past tense form of the verbs below.

1. vote _____

2. help _____

3. die _____

4. show _____

5. study _____

6. ask _____

7. need _____

8. compare _____

9. arrive _____

10. carry _____

B. Write the simple past tense of the verbs in parentheses.

1. They _____ (elect) a new president.

2. Native Americans _____ (help) the new settlers.

3. The Plains Indians _____ (dry) buffalo skins.

4. We _____ (learn) many things about using maps and charts.

5. I _____ (watch) the presidential debates on television last week.

6. The state representatives _____ (travel) to Philadelphia.

7. The Spanish sailors _____ (explore) new territory.

8. The Pony Express _____ (deliver) mail to the western settlers.

9. Our teacher _____ (list) the important events on a timeline.

10. The government _____ (want) more soldiers.

C. Rewrite the sentences. Use the simple past tense of the underlined verbs.

Example: The bar graph <u>shows</u> the same information as the line graph.

The bar graph showed the same information as the line graph.

1. The map key <u>helps</u> us find mountains, rivers, and cities.

_____

2. I <u>use</u> a globe to find the distance.

_____

3. We <u>study</u> how people, things, and ideas move.

_____

4. Students <u>locate</u> the pyramid on a map of Mexico.

_____

Negative Statements about the Past (Regular Verbs)

A. Change each past tense form to a negative.

Example: allowed ___*didn't allow*___

1. advised _____
2. warned _____
3. ordered _____
4. forced _____
5. signed _____

6. created _____
7. hurried _____
8. returned _____
9. lived _____
10. decided _____

B. Rewrite the sentences. Make each statement negative.

Example: The government helped the new settlers.

   ___*The government didn't help the new settlers.*___

1. The southern colonies wanted to end slavery.

   _____

2. The Germans invented the submarine.

   _____

3. The fighter planes destroyed Tokyo.

   _____

4. Columbus explored the New World for Portugal.

   _____

5. Lewis and Clark traveled across Colombia and Peru.

   _____

C. Complete the sentences. Use the negative past tense of the verbs in parentheses.

Example: The Aztecs ___*didn't celebrate*___ (celebrate) Thanksgiving.

1. Marco Polo _____ (visit) North America.
2. The Mexican Revolution _____ (happen) last year.
3. World War II _____ (end) in 1944.
4. Native Americans _____ (work) on plantations.
5. The United States _____ (export) rice last year.

Understanding the Past Tense

Simple Past Tense of Irregular Verbs

A. Write the simple past tense of the verbs in parentheses.

1. The Pilgrims _____ (come) to America a long time ago.

2. The Allies _____ (go) to war against the Germans.

3. Lewis and Clark _____ (draw) a map of their travels.

4. Native Americans _____ (have) to move to reservations.

5. The British _____ (fight) the colonists in the War for Independence.

6. The colonists _____ (win) their independence from England.

7. The slaves _____ (get) their freedom after the American Civil War.

8. The French _____ (give) assistance to the colonists.

9. Two atomic bombs _____ (fall) on Japan.

10. The Renaissance _____ (begin) in Italy.

B. Rewrite the sentences. Make each statement negative.

Example: People in early times knew the world was round.

People in early times didn't know the world was round.

1. People in Japan chose their emperor.

   _____

2. The Spanish explorers gave gold to the Aztecs.

   _____

3. The Egyptians bought the pyramids.

   _____

4. Most countries kept their colonies.

   _____

5. Juan Ponce de León found the Fountain of Youth.

   _____

C. Complete the sentences. Use *was* or *were*.

1. George Washington _____ the first president of the United States.

2. The Greeks and Romans _____ the rulers of the classical world.

3. Cleopatra _____ a queen of Egypt.

4. Early humans _____ hunter-gatherers.

5. The ancient Egyptians _____ the first people to use the 365-day calendar.

D. Rewrite each sentence as a *yes-no* question.

Example: I wrote the history essay last night.

Did you write the history essay last night?

1. I drew a map of Asia.

2. The South and the North fought in the American Civil War.

3. The Roman Empire had an emperor named Julius Caesar.

4. She thought geography was difficult.

5. The Portuguese brought the first slaves from Africa.

E. Rewrite each sentence as a *wh-* question.

Example: Columbus explored the Americas. (What?)

What did Columbus explore?

1. The Mayas left their temples. (What?)

2. The Great Depression began in 1929. (When?)

3. The Berlin Wall was in Germany. (Where?)

4. The Pilgrims left England to come to America. (Why?)

5. Many native people died because of European diseases. (Why?)

Understanding the Past Tense

Simple Past Tense: Regular and Irregular Verbs

A. Write the past tense form of each verb. Then write a sentence.

Example:

take *took*   *I took three tests yesterday.* _____

1. go _____ _____

2. stop _____ _____

3. live _____ _____

4. tell _____ _____

5. need _____ _____

6. help _____ _____

7. see _____ _____

8. say _____ _____

9. leave _____ _____

10. find _____ _____

B. Write the simple past tense of the verbs in parentheses.

Example: Bill Clinton _____ *was* _____ (be) an American president.

1. Frederick Douglass _____ (not agree) with slavery.

2. Neil Armstrong _____ (land) on the moon.

3. Leonardo da Vinci _____ (paint) the *Mona Lisa*.

4. Kings in Europe _____ (have) absolute power.

5. The United States _____ (be) part of the Industrial Revolution.

6. Chinese and Irish immigrants _____ (come) to America.

7. The United States government _____ (break) some of its treaties.

8. History is the study of things that _____ (happen) in the past.

9. We _____ (learn) many things in history.

10. The Romans _____ (not build) the pyramids.

C. Read the paragraph about Martin Luther King Jr. Complete the sentences with the correct past tense form of the verbs in parentheses.

Martin Luther King Jr. **(1)** _____ (be) born in 1929 in Atlanta, Georgia.

He **(2)** _____ (experience) racism while growing up in the South. At that

time, blacks and whites **(3)** _____ (not go) to the same schools. King

(4) _____ (attend) Morehouse College, and later **(5)** _____ (go)

to seminary school to become a minister. After he **(6)** _____ (graduate), he

(7) _____ (move) to Montgomery, Alabama. In the 1950s, King

(8) _____ (help) to start the Civil Rights movement. He **(9)** _____

(want) to improve the lives of African Americans in the United States. Later, he

(10) _____ (win) the 1964 Nobel Peace Prize. King **(11)** _____

(continue) to lead the Civil Rights movement, but on April 4, 1968, he

(12) _____ (die) in Memphis, Tennessee. He **(13)** _____ (be)

the victim of an assassination. Martin Luther King Jr. **(14)** _____ (become) a

national hero.

Understanding the Past Tense

Credits